LITERARY SYMBOLISM
A SYMPOSIUM

LITERARY SYMBOLISM

A SYMPOSIUM

❖━❖

Edited with an Introduction
by Helmut Rehder

Published for the Department of Germanic Languages of
the University of Texas by the

UNIVERSITY OF TEXAS PRESS, AUSTIN & LONDON

CONTENTS

ILLUSTRATIONS

(following page 98)

1. Multiplication, from S. Michelspacher, *Cabala, Spiegel der Kunst und Natur: In Alchymia* (1616)

2. Coniunction, from S. Michelspacher, *Cabala, Spiegel der Kunst und Natur: In Alchymia* (1616)

3. The "Twelfth Figure," from Lambspring, *Ein herrlicher teutscher Traktat vom philosophischen Steine* (1625)

4. Sargonid Seal (c. 2500 B.C.), Showing Shamash (sun god) Rising from Mountain

5. Sargonid Seal (c. 2500 B.C.), Showing Shamash (sun god) between Mountain Peaks

6. Babylonian World-Picture, Diagram from B. Meissner, *Babylonien und Assyrien*

7. Expulsion from Paradise, from the *Très Riches Heures du Duc de Berri*

8. Mountain of Purgatory, Illustration (15th century) to Dante, *Purgatorio* xxvii

INTRODUCTION

Symbolism

by

HELMUT REHDER

The University of Texas

INTRODUCTION

Symbolism

IN A WORLD where mutual understanding and intelligent communication have assumed greater importance than ever before, the selection of "symbolism" as the central topic of the fifth annual symposium of the Department of Germanic Languages at The University of Texas may occasion some doubts or some false anticipations. This choice of subject might create the suspicion that an outmoded theory of divination was to be rehabilitated where sober analysis is called for, or that logical reasoning was to assume a function ordinarily assigned to belief. Symbolism derives from a variety of conditions, forming a common basis of discussion for the five participants in the symposium. In language, or poetry, it may be a means of revealing the "truth" through images where words no longer possess an adequate power of expression; it may be the subtlest form of coincidence between referential and emotive utterance; and it may be simply a secret code for the initiated. In matters of social or individual behavior it may be the abdication of language and even of rational thinking in favor of primordial rituals, demonstrative actions, and sinister obscurantism. Purely as a means of expression, symbolism can be exclusive, threatening, and coldly demanding; it can be also inviting, comforting, and truly stimulative of the highest intellectual efforts.

The symbol as a mode of expression is peculiarly germane to primitive societies, and is closely associated with elemental experiences. Again, as the studied objective of literary art and criticism, it is particularly cultivated in eras of highly sensitive cultural self-consciousness. Almost without design, the following five essays deal with such an era comprising the two hundred years from Herder to recent German expressionism. It cannot be said that this era is characterized by an especially uniform intellectual physiognomy. Quite the opposite. Contemporary German poets are as indifferent toward nineteenth-century novelists as the rest of the Western world is toward post-Victorian sentimentalism. And yet the creative notions of a Novalis have brought about an unheralded resurrection of symbolism in modern times just as much as the poetic experiments of the aging Goethe—his "Classical Walpurgis Night," for example—anticipated the symbolic visions of later expressionists.

Some 160 years ago Friedrich Wilhelm Joseph Schelling, the author of romantic "Naturphilosophie," made the cryptic remark that "nature is the visible spirit" and "spirit is invisible nature," thereby attempting to formulate in a nutshell what, in retrospect, we might call "aesthetic pantheism,"—a cultured citizen's philosophy which sought, by means of the symbol, to bridge the gap between matter and mind, between existence and meaning. Schelling's tautological cliché was symptomatic of an atmosphere in which it was possible for romantic poets and solid burghers to exist side by side, sometimes ignoring, sometimes sneering at each other. With few exceptions, the pantheistic creed permeated the poetic production of nineteenth-century literature (including the German *Novelle,* whose symbolic practices Professor Remak has singled out for critical analysis). Its prevailing aesthetic attitude characterized the beliefs of many artists and scientists, enabling them, in their empirical attempts at capture or imitation of natural objects, to postulate, at least symbolically, an all-encompassing nature "behind" reality. Pantheism also induced Goethe to conclude his Faust poem with the praise of the symbol—"Alles Vergängliche ist nur ein Gleichnis" ("Everything mortal is merely symbolic.")—indicating, however, that the old dichotomy of matter and mind, existence and meaning, was still lingering on and that scientific inquiry is not silenced by the awesome intuition of the aesthetic symbol—the image of totality.

Today it may be said that pantheism is dead; it has been dead ever since Nietzsche pronounced the universality of the Dionysian urge; ever since the dynamism of social change began to determine the conception of individual freedom; or ever since physics intimated the hypothetical identity of matter and energy. To what extent modern dynamic criteria might be applied to Goethe's poetic efforts to resolve the phenomenon of change under the concept of Being is exemplified in Professor Jaszi's incisive observations on "Symbolism and the Linguistic Paradox." Within such a changed frame of reference the context of the symbol also has changed. As long as pantheism claimed to provide an adequate intuition of the whole, the image of totality suggested by the symbol was still "within" the world. But when existence is conceived of as a dynamism of changing forces, the reference of the symbol to changeless Being points "beyond" the world. It aims at transcendence at the risk of aiming at the void. The symbol has lost its aesthetically integrative force; it has lost its metaphysical appeal but has gained, as Professor Lehmann suggests, in its function as a logical, rational instrument in the ordering of "signs" —that is to say, in the manipulation of language.

The basic question, of course, remains: Has the symbol, which fulfilled a specific function in an age of belief and in the service of spiritual traditions, still retained, perhaps, its fundamental function in an age of science and technology, which to a large extent has made feasible and "makable," that is, comprehensible, what once was considered impossible for human achievement? Or has the process of separation and fragmentation, advancing to ever and ever smaller entities, succeeded in draining the concept of the symbol of its imaginative substance, thereby rendering it unsuitable for aesthetic purposes? As Professor Brinkmann points out, the disintegration of faith in reality in modern times is most strikingly reflected in a disintegration of language—"disintegration" from the point of view of traditional standards. On the other hand, the discovery of ever smaller particles and ever more minute processes in science, the fundamental revision of traditional time and space dimensions, the relativation of supposedly stable values has been accompanied by an awareness for ever-new and ever-changing complex relationships which, when mirrored in language, predicate an intensified experimentation with language itself, a new "experience into words." Just as the field of knowledge has been anatomized into innumerable areas of specialized inquiry, the theory of the symbol and of meaning has separated into numerous systems of "significant signs," many of which have often no more in common than the designation "symbolic." In a situation such as this, symbolism, which once served the purpose of aesthetic synthesis, has assumed the function of extreme differentiation in a manner in which the smallest entity, the particular, the unique event may be made transparent and comprehensible within a context of infinite references. And yet the emotive overtones in any symbol do not seem to admit that the symbol itself has paled with the growth of a highly differentiating scientific method of analysis, no matter what function the concept of "symbolic form" has been assigned in the logic of mathematics or psychology, anthropology or iconology, and many other disciplines. The significant feature common to all "symbolisms" appears to be the function of transition from observation to the signalization of meaning, from the rational to the incomprehensible.

Language, both as a physical phenomenon and as a carrier of meaning, is a particularly suitable medium for the analysis of symbolism; the analysis of *poetic* language is doubly rewarding since it comes closest, in the interpretation of literary works, to a possible analogy with the understanding of human individuals. As with the symbol, complete understanding of the individual is impossible; only signposts point in the direction of infinity. Scientific inquiry into the nature of these signposts has developed various methods. In our collection of essays the methods of linguistic and ontological analysis, iconological comparison, and historical and aesthetic criticism have been employed to the advantage of mutual complementation, and exclusion. The inherent characteristic of the symbol, its *momentary* manifestation of absolutes, can rarely be described in positive terms; and, even though the modern critic desires to be precise and specific and concrete, he abhors the rational precision of the allegory when distinguishing it from the arcanum of the symbol. For that reason he is reluctant, as Professor Middleton suggests, to apply traditional, "ready-made" meaning to the symbol, and looks for configurations which permit the "making of meaning" in the process of comprehension. In this process he is supported by linguistic analysis, which finds that meaning can result only from the sum total of contexts, for no single word possesses a "certain meaning."

In itself this very context may be unlimited, since it may well extend beyond the confines of a given text. Elements of the past are preserved in every symbol, coming down to us through the ages of mankind. Just as in the reality of nature every segment, even the minutest, carries an element that is both peculiarly concrete, because it belongs to the stuff of which the world is made, and peculiarly abstract, because it is subject to the mathematical formula of a natural law, so any poetic symbol may transcend beyond the private life of a poet and descend into the stuff and the laws of which human nature is made.

Most of the literary examples in this book derive from German literature and presuppose a certain knowledge of German poetic language. They do not exclude those readers whose interest in the nature of symbolism has prepared them for its immanent dialectics. Symbolism is a process of the imagination which originates in images, is carried forward by a sequence of images, and is projected into orbit by the dynamics of sequences. A symbol is that which represents a value in existence. But values cannot be described except by comparison and differentiation. Symbols do not have a counterpart in experience. They are therefore configurations which stand for a reality that we cannot imagine.

This symposium on symbolism was meant to contribute to the discovery of consonance in the diversities of the symbol, to examine it, in the words of Jacques Maritain, as the sign which is the keystone of the life of the mind.

THE STONY IDIOM OF THE BRAIN

Symbolic Manipulation of Language in Literature

—❧—

by
W. P. LEHMANN
The University of Texas

THE STONY IDIOM OF THE BRAIN

Symbolic Manipulation of Language in Literature

THROUGHOUT most of Western culture literature sets out to be an imitation of nature, of life. However one may interpret mímēsis, in the works of Plato, Aristotle, and their successors,[1] the career of Achilles quite credibly imitates that of a young hero, and has itself been imitated, by heroes and by authors. After Freud we accept the strange relationships of the Oedipus household as possible even in families less troubled than Eugene O'Neill's. And Ariel sipping where the bee sips, the child frightened by the Erlkönig, are earthly if somewhat imaginative beings. Actions, characters, words of this literature mime life, whether the poet speaks in his own person, whether he speaks through his characters, or whether he and the characters both speak. This central convention—the axiom that literature imitate nature—was maintained through several millennia of Western literature, but broken during the last century, most sharply by the literary figures known as "symbolists."

Like the term "literature," symbolism generally has been defined

[1] A highly important discussion for the general purposes of literary criticism is the essay of Richard McKeon, "Literary Criticism and the Concept of Imitation in Antiquity," first published in *Modern Philology,* 34 (August, 1936), 1–35, and reprinted with changes in *Critics and Criticism: Ancient and Modern,* ed. by R. S. Crane (Chicago: University of Chicago Press, 1952; now Phoenix Book P 15). Since paperback reprints are most generally accessible, references will be made to them, even when, as here, they are abridged editions. No single quotation could do justice to its usefulness; of especial pertinence here is the statement included in McKeon's discussion of Aristotle's use of "imitation": "The object of imitation is the actions of men" (P 15.133).

by its ends rather than its means. For Edmund Wilson[2] the symbolist shifts "the field of literature . . . from an objective to a subjective world" just as Count Axel of Auersberg rejected the world in favor of his isolated castle (259 ff.). Symbolism itself Wilson defined (21–22) "as an attempt by carefully studied means—a complicated association of ideas represented by a medley of metaphors—to communicate unique personal feelings."

Though their means may have been less studied, poets, especially lyric poets, have always tried to "communicate unique personal feelings"; Goethe does not say, "Wie herrlich leuchtet *uns* die Natur." Nor are metaphors, or even symbols, found only in symbolists. In his introduction to symbolism, Symons had admitted for it "no value if it were not seen also, under one disguise or another, in

---

[2] References are to Edmund Wilson's "study in the imaginative literature of 1870–1930," *Axel's Castle* (New York: Charles Scribner's Sons, 1931).

The bibliography on symbolism is vast and can scarcely be suggested here. In addition to Wilson's book, a good introduction is Joseph Chiari, *Symbolisme from Poe to Mallarmé: The Growth of a Myth* (London: Rockliff, 1956), especially for its discussion of underlying aesthetic principles and commentary on the interrelationship between Poe and Mallarmé, between American and French literature.

Symbolism and American Literature, by Charles Feidelson, Jr. (Chicago: University of Chicago Press, 1953; now Phoenix Book P 37), discusses American symbolist literature of the nineteenth century, especially Hawthorne, Whitman, Melville, and Poe, and indicates the generality of the departure from an "imitation of nature," as in a quotation from Whitman (P 37.3): "No useless attempt to repeat the material creation, by daguerreotyping the exact likeness by mortal mental means." It is remarkable that the superiority of the camera over the painter in capturing exact likenesses should have been recognized so early in its implications for the other arts.

Contrasting with these in examining the symbol as such, rather than its varying role for successive literary figures, is William York Tindall, *The Literary Symbol* (*LS.* New York: Columbia University Press, 1955; now Midland Book 7).

The most influential general statement is Ernst Cassirer's *Philosophie der symbolischen Formen,* especially Vol. 1, *Die Sprache* (Berlin: B. Cassirer, 1923); even though its views on language are often unpalatable for contemporary linguists. The English translation by Ralph Manheim (New Haven: Yale University Press, 1953) contains an excellent introduction by Charles W. Hendel, which also discusses Cassirer's relationship to literary figures like Herder and Goethe.

I should also like to acknowledge the assistance of Mr. Jerome Bunnag, of the Linguistics Research Center, The University of Texas.

every great imaginative writer."[3] But can we, like Symons, recognize as the distinctive characteristic of the "symbolism of our day . . . that it has now become conscious of itself"? "Conscious of itself" for what goal—"to create my own universe around me," like Nerval, "to whom [Symons] traces the particular origin of the literature which [he] calls Symbolist"?

And how create one's own universe—by a Mallarméian veil of smoke, by walls of cork, by a medley of metaphors? The means are closer at hand, indicated to us in one of our ancient texts. If God could say, "Let there be light," and there was light, and if "in the beginning . . . the word . . . abstracted all the letters of the void . . . from the solid bases of the light"[4] (CP 27), language might again create a world. With language a poet might make his own heaven and earth—he might cooperate with God in creating the Universe.[5] But the language could not be that of the farm, the market, the laboratory. A poet would have to manipulate his own speech to produce "first characters of birth and death." When he did, his poetry would not imitate nature. The object imitated was language itself.

The essence of symbolism accordingly is a new molding of its medium, its characteristic manipulation of language. The symbolist did not freshen or extend his language by drawing from neglected resources. Luther may have gone to the market to find appropriate terms to represent the broad subject matter of the Bible; Wordsworth found in the countryside unspoiled speech to bring new life past the formal rhetoric of poetry in his time; later Zola may look to the scientist for means to represent activities with greater precision, a procedure recently recommended by Huxley.[6] But for the symbolist

[3] Cf. Arthur Symons, *The Symbolist Movement in Literature* (London: W. Heinemann, 1899), edited by Richard Ellmann (*SML.* New York: E. P. Dutton & Co., Inc., 1958; Dutton Paperback D 21), p. 2.

[4] Quotations are from *The Collected Poems of Dylan Thomas* 1934–1953, a New Directions Book. Page numbers are indicated after *CP*.

[5] See Symons' quotation from Nerval, *SML* 6: "I do not ask of God that he should change anything in events themselves, but that he should change me in regard to things, so that I might have the power to create my own universe about me . . ." Also Tindall, *LS* 46–47: "The French symbolists used symbol not so much to unite worlds as to create them . . ."

[6] Aldous Huxley, *Literature and Science* (London: Harper & Row, 1963).

it was essential to create an individual language, to draw from himself an idiom which would enable him to express his feelings with directness and immediacy.

What led to this insistence on framing a new, individual language, to the "progressive dissociation of language from experience" as it has seemed (*Times Literary Supplement* 3210, September 6, 1963, p. 667)? In the late eighteenth century poets set out to make a "selection of language really used by men."[7] The language of "humble and rustic life" was chosen by Wordsworth for his poems "because, in that condition, the essential passions of the heart . . . speak a plainer and more emphatic language." Moreover, "such men hourly communicate with the best objects from which the best part of language is originally derived." Whatever Wordsworth thought this best part to be, Herder esteemed the language of early man because it was "sinnlich," and he modeled on it his own style— as Eric Blackall has recently pointed out.[8] While Wordsworth brought poetry back to the "more permanent, and . . . far more philosophical language" of rustic life, Herder believed that poetry had retained a capability to communicate more directly than do other forms of language, and accordingly poetry is the *oratio perfecta sensitiva*.

These sources for a more emphatic language did not fulfil their promise; a short time later Hoffmann looked elsewhere for a more perfect and sensitive means of expression. Like Herder he held that man's capacity for communication has deteriorated, but for him "painting and music had not lost their directness of feeling to the same extent as had poetry."[9] Beethoven, the pure romantic com-

---

[7] Quotations are from Wordsworth's *Preface to Lyrical Ballads.*

[8] Herder's comments on language have been as widely discussed as they have been influential, even on one of the founders of contemporary linguistic theory, E. Sapir. In "The Imprint of Herder's Linguistic Theory on his Early Prose Style" *PMLA*, 76 (December, 1961), 512–518, Eric A. Blackall has indicated how Herder somewhat like the symbolists related his practice to his theory. Blackall also cites influences on Herder, e.g. Baumgarten's definition of poetry as *oratio perfecta sensitiva.*

[9] The views of Hoffmann represented here are taken from his *Dichtungen und Schriften,* 15 vols., ed. by Walter Harich (Weimar: E. Lichtenstein, 1924). For this comment on his views of painting and music versus poetry see W. Harich, *E. T. A. Hoffmann* (Berlin: E. Reiss, 1920), 1.108.

poser, for example, seemed to Hoffmann less successful in his music for voice than in his instrumental music (12.237). For Hoffmann, whose works were well-known to Poe—the idol of the French symbolists—"the mysterious language of a distant spiritual kingdom (*Geisterreich*), whose marvelous accents resound within us and awaken a higher intense life" (13.107) is music. Penetrating to the "blessedness of that distant paradise," we find that the poet and the musician are "intimately related members of one church"—for the secret of word and tone is the same (13.106). But since the word has fallen from its mysterious eminence, our most perfect communication is through tone.

Hoffmann's may be the world of Ulalume—but in spite of the admiration of Baudelaire and his successors for Poe, it is not the universe of the symbolist. Poe, like Hoffmann, may have equated tone and word, but he did it by divesting the word of its rational meaning, by reducing it to a component of music. For the symbolist, language is not merely a succession of pleasant sounds, a sensuous form of expression. His symbols are not selected because they are made up of pleasant sequences of *r*'s or *l*'s, of *o*'s or *u*'s. They are rather "images pregnant with signification"—which must be fashioned by the poet and every other artist. Like language for Cassirer, they are "*at once* a sensuous and an intellectual form of expression."[10]

In the developing recognition that a new manipulation of language was essential, the role of the late romantics was negative. Having abandoned the quest for a purer, directer form of language which may have survived in a rustic Arcadia, in their pessimism they turned to pure sound—to the expressive possibilities of music. For "only the composer has penetrated into the secrets of harmony, able through it to have an effect on the spirit of man; the musical proportions, which remain dead, rigid computational problems to the grammarian lacking genius, are for him magical preparations out of which he produces a mysterious world" (Hoffmann, 12.240). If, however, the mysterious world seems inadequate, if man wishes to

---

[10] See Hendel's Introduction to *The Philosophy of Symbolic Forms* by Ernst Cassirer (1.50).

comprehend the *mundus intelligibilis* as well as the *mundus sensibilis,* the abstract expression of the musician too is inadequate.

The poet must devise his own language to meet the needs of the senses and of the intellect. The design is determined by the symbolists' view of the world and man's access to it.

Their view is ultimately Kantian: that "human knowledge is not shaped to reality; rather, human judgment determines whatever is to have the character of being reality . . ." (Hendel, 6). If "judgment is reality," then man's sensations are reflections of a "small number of ideas, of *Mütter.*"[11] It is the poet's task to select among these and produce verbal syntheses. For Goethe "the eternal is to be seen in the transitory" (Hendel, 31). A poem depicts a selected experience, whether on the lake, at a special occasion, in a passing mood. But as the language of ordinary life was inadequate for the symbolists in representing the absolute, the eternal, so a selection from experience failed to reveal it. Rather, the symbolist poet arrays related sensations which reflect the Absolute, represents these in a sequence of words with a special rhythm to form a poem, "a total word, new, foreign to the language and like an incantation."[12] In Rilke's words, "Gesang ist Dasein" *(Sonette an Orpheus* I.3.7)

Every poem then is a tiny language. Yet presumably the successive poems of one poet share to some extent sensations, symbols, and other idiosyncratic devices. If so, a poem may be viewed as one phase, or even as a dialect of the total language of a poet. As dialects may

---

[11] This relationship between the "mothers" of Goethe and the sensations for which symbolist poets seek to find symbols is suggested by A.-M. Schmidt, *La Littérature symboliste,* Vol. 82 in Que sais-je? (Paris: Presses Universitaires de France, 1960), p. 55. It is curious that in the Tenth Duino Elegy the last vision shown the dead man is the constellation "m" that symbolizes *Mütter:* "Aber im südlichen Himmel, rein wie im Inneren einer gesegneten Hand, das klar ergänzende 'm,' das die Mütter bedeutet." Benn on the other hand speaks disparagingly of the attempt to relate everything to the *Mütter.* Cf. *Der Dichter und das Gedicht.* Cf. Gottfried Benn, Gesammelte Werke (Wiesbaden: Limes Verlag, 1959, 1962²), I. 508 (reference to *Mütter*); I, 533–536 (Rede in Darmstadt). See also Schmidt, p. 6: "Baudelaire, en effet, est convaincu que nul, parmi les objets modestes ou grandioses de l'univers, ne possède de réalité propre. Il n'a d'existence perceptible que pour manifester ce que la mesquine parole humaine se résigne à nommer une idée."

[12] Like many of the proclamations of the symbolists this one of Mallarmé's has been cited repeatedly.

resemble each other closely, or differ widely, so may poems. Almost parenthetically, if the poems of one symbolist poet may be studied together as are a number of dialects, so the poems of a succession of poets may resemble a number of languages in one stock, and be examined and clarified for similarities and differences. But our fundamental precept for understanding symbolist verse must be that if symbolists construct new languages, if the essence of symbolism was that poets through an intuitive understanding of language imitated it rather than nature, then our procedures for understanding their verse may resemble those used in understanding language.

Oddly enough, in spite of its central position in our activities, language is a mystery to most of us—and obscure in much of its operation to everyone, so that some discussion of its functioning is not idle. For until recently, like most human and natural activities, it was taken for granted rather than examined.[13] Humanists, whose concern is and has been language, may console themselves by recalling that natural scientists began to examine the natural phenomenon "fire" only a few centuries ago; the less cheerful, or more wearied, humanist may find even greater solace in noting that fire, like language, came to be an object of sustained inquiry when its manipulation was industrially of interest.

Passing over details, we may locate within the present century an accurate, nonintuitive understanding of the functioning of language and the start of procedures which enable us to analyze it adequately. Within forty years after the publication of Saussure's lecture notes on linguistics, everyone agrees that language is a "system of signs"; implications of this definition may be vague except from examples. The question

What is the mátter with the dictionary?

[13] The situation of philosophy is comparable. See Gilbert Ryle, "The Theory of Meaning," *British Philosophy in the Mid-Century,* ed. C. A. Mace (London: George Allen and Unwin, Ltd., 1957), reprinted in *The Importance of Language,* ed. M. Black (a Spectrum Book S 37; Englewood Cliffs, New Jersey, 1962), pp. 162–163: "Until fairly recently philosophers have not often stepped back from their easels to consider what philosophy is . . ." Saussure may be credited for determining the activities of linguistics, particularly through the ideas published in his posthumous book, *Cours de linguistique générale* (third edition; Paris: Payot, 1949).

may be taken as a typical English utterance, one possibly not infrequent in certain circles after the publication of the Third International. We could vary this question in a number of minimal ways, but suppose we contrast it with a possibly startling but still acceptable question:

What is the matter with the diction, Mary?

Here we have added one entity, an /m/; with modifications in the sentence intonation this addition changes completely the situation called up by the question. Somewhat less than the difference between these two utterances—possibly—would be that between the last and

What is the matter with the diction, Barry?

The signs which lead us to recognize the difference are the consonants /m/ and /b/.

It is a strange fact about language that these smallest of its signs have no meaning; they participate in shaping more extensive signs like *Mary, Barry, Terry,* which have meaning. But it is quite pointless even to speculate what the *m*-ness of /m/ might be. Only one conclusion is possible from the different roles of entities like /m/ and others like {Mary} in the language: that language consists of various levels, different strata, each having different entities and different rules for their arrangement. The recognition that a language is a multilevel structure is of great importance for the understanding of symbolist poetry, as for that of any verse or any text.

A second fact about the structuring of language also has particular relevance for symbolist poetry. Its signs operate as much negatively as by positive reference. By using /m/ before /eriy/ I exclude all other possible names: *Barry, Terry, Cary, Gary,* and so on; at the same time of course I specify one. But if *I* had two friends, one with the name ⟨Merry⟩, the other with the name ⟨Mary⟩, I have no way of excluding one of them in my speech. If I had learned my English in New York State, I probably would—calling the first /mériy/, the second /méyriy/. Our way of interpreting utterances by exclusion has important consequences for "meaning." Obviously *my* utterance /mériy/ has broader meaning than do the two possibilities /mériy/ and /méyriy/ of some speakers. For my set of names ending in /riy/ is smaller. The meaning of words is determined in a number of ways, one by the size of the set to which they belong. If I use a language with three names for the set of colors we label: *violet indigo blue green yellow orange red,* the meanings of the three names are broader than the English seven; in a language with two, roughly "light" and "dark," the meanings are still broader.[14] In somewhat the same manner as this last language, I may choose to restrict my possibilities in my own language: I may for special purposes, whether linguistic or scientific, or poetic, establish sets with small numbers of members. If I do, the meanings of these members will be correspondingly modified—and they will be regulated by the sets to which they belong.

Before we examine the implications of this functioning of language for symbolist poetry we may observe how we determine meanings, allowing some possibilities, excluding others.

Returning to our original question we may vary it in a way that may seem a bit bookish or old-fashioned, but is still an acceptable English utterance:

What is the matter of the dictionary?

In this utterance *matter* has an entirely different meaning from that in:

What is the matter with the dictionary?

Yet we have not modified it, substituting /b/ for /m/ or changing any of its components. Rather, we have modified its surroundings. In our bookish question *matter* means "stuff" because it is accompanied by *of*; and in our first question it means "trouble," "shortcoming" because it is accompanied by *with*. These are surroundings of grammatical entities which reveal through restriction the meaning of *matter*. Restrictions may also be introduced by physical surroundings: In a hospital, *matter* may refer to bodily discharge; in other surroundings it may have other meanings, even to virtually the opposite of its general meaning in a meeting of Christian Scientists, for

[14] See the discussion in H. A. Gleason, *An Introduction to Descriptive Linguistics* (New York: H. H. Rinehart and Winston, 1961), pp. 4–5.

whom *matter* may be the "unreal."[15] In normal discourse we are fairly sure of our grammatical and physical surroundings; accordingly the meaning of an utterance may be quite clear. If we are dealing with symbolist verse, on the other hand, the poet determines both the physical and the grammatical surroundings—as well as the grammatical sets: in the verse of Cummings, *am* may be a noun. He is introducing us to a new universe in which only the basic shell is unchanged—the sounds and many of the grammatical rules. In this universe our question may be:

What is the metre of the dictionary?

What can we do with such a question? What could Dylan Thomas have had in mind? By one substitution from a possible prosaic question, without introducing any unusual pattern at the lower levels of language, including syntax, he confronts us with apparent nonsense.[16] Or does *metre* not mean what it does in reference to a poem? Is a *dictionary* here not a list of forms with definitions?

If *metre* and *dictionary* have anything like their normal meanings, they are probably instances of the long line of symbols based on books and writing, including the "book . . . sealed with seven seals . . . in the right hand of him that sat on the throne" (*Revelations* 5.1).

---

[15] See the definition of *matter* in *Webster's Third New International Dictionary* (Springfield: G. & C. Merriam Company, 1963).

[16] This is not the place, nor the time, to review the various interpretations of the sonnet cycle. I am in close sympathy with E. Olson, *The Poetry of Dylan Thomas* (*PDI*) (Chicago: University of Chicago Press, 1954; also Phoenix Book P 72). Yet I will not indicate departures from Olson's views, nor compare others, like C. Emery, *The World of Dylan Thomas* (Coral Gables: University of Miami Press, 1962), or H. H. Kleinman, *The Religious Sonnets of Dylan Thomas* (Berkeley: University of California Press, 1963). If any support were needed for the symbolist view that the poet merely sets the stage without specifying precisely his meaning, the varying views of critics would supply it. Although dogmatism of every kind must be avoided in dealing with symbolist poets, I should like to suggest that the chief critical pitfall is an attempt to find a simple or a single meaning in symbolist verse, one with no contradictions. For example, Emery finds difficulties in Olson's astronomical frame for the sonnets (*World of Dylan Thomas* 214 ff), expecting noncontradictory reflections, and also more general use of astronomical stuff in Thomas' poetry if this frame is posited for the sonnets. But Rilke borrows even more remotely in his *Sonette an Orpheus,* relying in I.11 and in the last of the *Duino Elegien* on Arabic astronomy.

Especially since they came to view language as a pattern for constructing their own idiom, poets have treated it like a metalanguage, mining it for special terms, for symbols. For Hoffmann the grammarian is a figure who sees the world of harmony made up of rigid proportions. And "from the first declension of the flesh . . ." Dylan Thomas learnt

> man's tongue, to twist the shapes of thoughts
> Into the stony idiom of the brain,
> To shade and knit anew the patch of words
> Left by the dead . . . (25.8)

If the universe is a language, if life has grammar, flesh has declensions (25.7), blood may be syllabic (19.8), words may walk (Sonnet 1.11), verbs of will may yield a secret (25.15) and the sum total of life may be a dictionary. As selected sequences of language may have meter, so may segments of life.

Sonnet IV starts with this general question:

> What is the pattern of life?

and then moves to specific details. Among segments of life, what is:

> The size of genesis—(the dimensions of origin)
> the short spark's gender—(the sex of the seed)
> Shade without shape?—(the soul without form)
> the shape of Pharaoh's echo?—(the form of Cepheus' echo)

After these three lines of questions about life in its beginnings, Thomas adds a fourth in parentheses, a commentary on the poet's role here (or, as Olson prefers, the poetic character's):

> (My shape of age nagging the wounded whisper)

the mature man asking questions about the faint whispers of beginning life.

Earlier we stated that like language symbolist poetry consists of a series of strata, with various meanings conveyed at the various strata. We may again use paraphrases to illustrate.

By changing the lowest level, that of sound, including intonation,

> This is the metre of the dictionary

differs from

> This is the métre of the dictionary.

By changing the next level, that of form, we further modify meaning, as in

> Thís is the metre of the dictionaries.

By changing the order, or syntax, we introduce still more modifications of meaning: Is thís the metre of the dictionaries? As we move to further levels we do not forfeit the meaning at lower levels, but modify it in various ways, building up a hierarchical structure.

In a similar way, a symbolist poet may manipulate various strata of symbols. Olson identified the following types of symbolism in the sonnets (*PDT* 64):

1. one based on the analogy of human life to the span of a year
2. one based on the analogy between the sun and man
3. one based on "private" symbolism
4. one based on ancient myth, relating the sun to the sun-hero Hercules
5. one based on the relations of the constellation Hercules to other constellations
6. one based on Christian interpretations of Strata 4 and 5.

If, however, symbolic verse is like language, the strata are not merely coexistent—they are also hierarchical: one is built on another, takes its stuff from the other, maintaining the meaning of lower strata though with modifications. Olson's six types must accordingly be rearranged in a hierarchy, for obviously they are not parallel.

Of the symbolic hierarchy, the lowest is taken from a poet's experience, his private symbols. Those of Thomas revolve around raw life, sex, the sea; Benn, Verlaine, and others have their own sources, such as Benn's well-known manipulation of medical terms. For any symbolist poet we must mark the key private symbols and undertake to interpret them as the lowest stratum of his symbolic structure.

Such are the symbols in the first three lines of Sonnet IV. "Pharaoh's echo" leads us to Thomas' next stratum, that based on myth. Like his private symbolism, the general symbolism of a poet may have various sources: Yeats' is largely Celtic story; Thomas' source is primarily classical mythology and the Bible, especially the mystical books. This stratum is complex. It is not at all difficult to interpret with Olson "Pharaoh" as Cepheus, the King of Ethiopia, the husband of Cassiopeia and father of Andromeda, combining Biblical with classical story. But in addition, when we shift to Cepheus we are in the heavens, among the constellations—which have varied meanings for pagan and for Christian. In Sonnet V the relationships of the northern constellations, as Olson excellently indicates, are reflected in detail. Sonnet IV merely flashes hints on the general topic of the sonnet sequence.

For in Sonnet IV the poet is speaking almost discursively, he is almost argufying, in contrast with the pure symbols of the following sonnets. Set in the heavens, line 5

> Which sixth of wind blew out the burning gentry?

takes us to Revelations 6.12: "And I beheld when he had opened the sixth seal, and, lo, there was a great earthquake; and the sun became black as sackcloth of hair, and the moon became as blood; And the stars of heaven fell unto the earth, even as a fig tree casteth her untimely figs, when she is shaken of a mighty wind." Through this reference we are confronted with the end of the world, with questions of death to the living essence, or as Thomas says:

> (Questions are hunchbacks to the poker marrow.)

What is the role in life of the bamboo man—Death? Can one escape him, corseting the graveyards, or buttoning a bodice on dead bones? The answer is so apparent that Thomas merely presents man's solution: the Christian triumphant in the face of apparent impossibilities will ultimately make his way through the bodice, the shroud. For him a camel may pass through the eye of a needle, defeating death. Lines 5 through 10 in this way allude to the portents before the Judgment Day of Revelations 6, to man's inability to evade death, but also to his ultimate victory. As in Revelations the effects resulting from the opening of the sixth seal were checked by the angel ascending from the east, so in Sonnet IV the power of death will be overcome by the needle of the Christian.

What is the metre of the dictionary?
The size of genesis? the short spark's gender?
Shade without shape? the shape of Pharaoh's echo?
(My shape of age nagging the wounded whisper).
Which sixth of wind blew out the burning gentry?
(Questions are hunchbacks to the poker marrow).
What of a bamboo man among your acres?
Corset the boneyards for a crooked boy?
Button your bodice on a hump of splinters,
My camel's eyes will needle through the shrowd.
Love's reflection of the mushroom features,
Stills snapped by night in the bread-sided field,
Once close-up smiling in the wall of pictures,
Arc-lamped thrown back upon the cutting flood.

Dealing with the end of life in lines 5 through 10, as opposed to its beginning in lines 1 through 4, Thomas manipulates higher, complex strata of symbols. Yet the lower is not abandoned. *Marrow*, from Thomas' private stratum, contrasts with the *hunchback*, as do *poker*, and *needle*; the *crook* contrasts with the splintered *hump* of death. Such symbols from the private stratum are here arranged in smaller but more comprehensive sets of a higher stratum. Mingled with both is a stratum based on astronomical and religious symbols. The intertwining of reliance on constellation, Christian, and mythical imagery for the sonnet is variously apparent: 1) in the reference to Cepheus, king of spots; 2) in the allusion to the Queen in splints, Cassiopeia, the Queen with a shuffled heart; 3) in the play on Cameleopardus, the constellation which with a camel's eye, later a seaeye (VI.5), follows Cepheus and Cassiopeia through the northern skies. All strata as yet provide an indistinct picture: the symbol of life's triumph over death is the eye of the humped beast. But since at this stage of the sonnets the emphasis is on Christian rather than astronomical symbolism, the biblical reference "camel's eyes" is most explicit. Still the poet only hints of the answer to his questions about life and death.

Before we move on to the last four lines of the sonnet, to the indistinct picture which the camel's eyes see, we return to questions of method. We noted above that meaning is determined by contrasts, that in ascertaining it we must posit sets (like the set of the colors of the rainbow). The primary set here at a higher stratum is simply life and death. Characteristics reflect the pair negatively and positively. Life burns like the stars, is straight, corseted, buttoned, vital as marrow; death is the wind that blows out the stars, hunched, crooked, splintered—like bamboo, empty as marrowless bone. Questions reflect death; the question mark is itself hunchbacked. As the camel's eyes needle through the shroud, therefore, the spate of questions ceases; and for the rest of the sonnet, indeed for the rest of the sequence with one exception—when in the last comes a passing reference to man returning from death to life—no questions arise, their absence indicating the poet's growing confidence in the victory of life over death.

His confidence is very dim, however, in Sonnet IV. The eyes see only love's reflection of the features of life—the mushroom, the Milky Way; only still shots taken by night, if in the field bordered by life-giving manna; and only once a smiling close-up on the whole wall of pictures. Rather than sharp, distinct photographs, unedited frames are produced by a projector on a motion-picture screen.

Olson's commentary on the sonnet sequence is so fundamental to an understanding of them that I shun criticism. Yet his interpretation of the last four lines may illuminate the necessity of our third principle of interpretation—determination of meaning by contexts (cf. p. 18 above). Of these lines Olson says (*PDT* 73): "So the poet had once imagined God as speaking through the stars; this was how, in the mirror of his love, the features of the stars had appeared to him, glimpsed for a moment or so, 'like stills snapped,' . . ." In their context, however, the last four lines must indicate what the *camel's eyes* saw; unless we take these to be God's, which I do not, the vision is the poet's. As the cinematic terms *arc-lamped* and *cutting* prepare for the motion-picture entrance of Gabriel in the following sonnet, so the context *eyes* directs our interpretation of lines 11 through 14.

In commenting on this sonnet I have not been primarily interested in proposing a total interpretation, nor in contesting available commentaries, nor even in examining Thomas' individual mode of writing, but rather in the techniques which are useful for dealing with symbolist verse. I have also excluded comments on Thomas' manipulation of sound, rime, assonance, rhythm—of forms and syntax, his use of nouns, verbs, adjective phrases, and the like—for analysis of these is mandatory in all verse. A fine example of the relation between syntactic structure and content is available in the last four lines of the sonnet: they are not assertions, not complete sentences, simply a series of phrases strung along, illustrating again the poet's uncertainty at this point in the sonnet cycle.[17] The essential requirement for understanding symbolism is a special technique of managing the symbols; this technique must be based on the reflection of language characteristic of symbolic verse. Just as we manipulate language as a series of signs arranged in hierarchies, whose entities have meanings determined by contrasts in accordance with their contexts, so the

[17] I should like to think that Thomas for this reason modified the original form of the line from *Love's a reflection* to *Love's reflection*.

symbolist poet produces verse consisting of series of symbols arranged in hierarchies.

We must observe that the hierarchical manipulation of symbols has nothing to do with the widely practiced variety of interpretations of a text to which we all are accustomed. We have been taught to read biblical passages, and some other writings, for their literal, allegorical, moral, and anagogical senses. If we consider the sonnets in the visionary tradition, and choose to determine these "four senses" we must do so at every stratum of the symbols.

That symbolists used symbols differently from previous writers has been recognized and needs no further discussion.[18] Accordingly we must apply to their writings different principles of interpretation.

Further illustrations of these principles of interpretation could be taken from various symbolist poets, or from various writings of Thomas. In view of the difficulties of symbolist verse, it may be help-ful to remain with the sonnets. In line 12 of Sonnet IV *bread-sided field* has a special meaning, for *bread,* as elsewhere in Thomas, is God's bread, furnished to the chosen, manna (*PDT* 73). Accord-ingly the field is the heavens. The heavens are the areas of the con-stellations, including Hercules, who in the myth represents the sun, a figure of man. The *stills snapped* are then incidents in the life of man. *Bread* in this way conveys special meaning in Thomas' private and mythical strata of symbols. The assertion hardly needs support that *bread* here belongs to a different set of symbols from one that might make use of Fitzgerald's often cited line. Moreover, the meaning is underlined by the context: the previous line had dealt with *mush-room features,* a symbolic synonym for Thomas of food, milk, The Milky Way (*PDT* 67).

For an example of meaning determined by contexts outside the cycle we may take a phrase from Sonnet V, *by the hair* in the line:

And Jonah's Moby snatched me by the hair

[18] See for example Wilson, *Axel's Castle* 20: "For the symbols of Symbolism have to be defined a little differently from symbols in the ordinary sense . . ." In his influential monograph, however, Symons attempted to illustrate con-tinuity with the past by prefacing a quotation from Carlyle: "It is in and through Symbols that man, consciously or unconsciously, lives, works, and has his being: those ages, moreover, are accounted the noblest which can the best recognise symbolical worth, and prize its highest."

which seems to Olson a pun on the constellation Lepus, the Hare, and a reference to Absolom. But among the events after the opening of the sixth seal in Revelations 6.12, "the sun became black as sackcloth of hair." Clearly the constellation Cetus, the Whale, seizes a sun (Hercules in his [black] suit of spades) who has characteristics of the constellation of Greek myth and of Christian vision.

At this point the question may be asked whether such frightful complexity is designed—whether the untutored or primitive Thomas would produce verse the understanding of which requires a broad grasp of astronomical, classical, and Christian lore. The best answer, as with any text, is consistency and completeness of interpretation. If Olson demonstrates a consistent use of the northern constellations and those traversed by the sun as the underlying structural bond of the sonnets, we can hardly assert that Thomas hadn't designed it. We know how he worked—how the apparently difficult "Ballad of the Long-legged Bait" follows the pattern of Rimbaud's "Bateau ivre" (Tindall, *LS* 155); we may then accept a similar procedure of work for the sonnets, with the essentials here following the Book of Revelations and various mythological and astronomical texts. The problem of difficulty in literary works has been amply discussed, also with regard to Thomas.[19] Those who prefer simple verse have ready possibilities in that dealing with a tree, or a swing, or even a Grecian urn. If a contemporary poet who wishes to comment on the cycle of life considers his task from the point of view of his audience, he had better be aware that some of them have absorbed the work of Frazer, of Freud, have superimposed it on their classical and Christian traditions. But what of the reader who hasn't? Or what about the assertion that symbols have varying significance for various speakers, and accordingly "a symbolist work has no certain meaning"? (Tindall, *LS* 267).

One achievement of a poet like Thomas is his conveyance of meaning at all levels. It is quite certain that the large audiences who heard him recite his verse had only a dim understanding of its impli-

[19] See *PDT* 36–37, 45–47, e.g., 46–47: "Why should a poet be thus deliberately difficult? . . . Obscurity . . . is a device; and one obvious use of it is to force the reader to give a poem the close attention it requires . . ."

cations, of its intellectual content. Suppose we look at a line from
Sonnet IV:

> What sixth of wind blew out the burning gentry?

For Olson *sixth* was selected because the wind might blow out the
stars from the four cardinal directions, from above or below, with
further implications. I have suggested that the number reflects the
vision in Revelations. But suppose we look at Thomas' possibilities
at the simplest stratum, the phonological, among the numerals: a
/fft/ or /fift/ of wind would scarcely do more than blow out a
candle; a *fourth* or *third* would have scatological implications for
any Thomas adept. The other numerals are equally unsatisfactory;
only *sixth* has the clean brisk sound of an adequate wind. Even if the
audience didn't think of the natural possibilities or of the literary
forebears, *sixth* by its very sound makes a fine line.

To pursue the problem of variety of meaning: what segment of
language does not have it? What is "bread" to you? The crusty,
delicious Turkish bread, wheaty, with a possible tang from the old
method of threshing grain, hence "Guernsey bread"—the sturdy,
meaty bread designed to take a Norwegian through a vigorous day
of trudging through the damp chill of one season or skiing in the crisp
air of another—or something else? If so, what is the "certain meaning" of bread in its literal sense for you and me, not to speak of its
meaning for John reporting Jesus as "the bread of life" or for
Thomas? To a linguist no words have a certain meaning; their
meaning for each of us is the sum total of the contexts in which they
have occurred for us; it is scarcely necessary to expand on the unique-
ness of these for every individual. From this point of view the prime
task of the symbolist poet is to find relevant symbols of comparable
meaning to a wide audience; his aim is to find more certain meanings than you and I apply in a prosaic statement such as "I don't
like bread."

The symbolist poet is therefore an explorer of language—only one
of the broad band who in the nineteenth century set out to pull
apart, test, and remodel man's means of communication: philologists
considered the best area an understanding of the earliest historical
stages of language, ancient Germanic, Greek, Sanskrit, even Indo-

European; mathematicians looked to the structure of the sentence, substituting Boolean symbols and formulae for the old logical paradigms (Socrates was a man—men are mortal—etc.); physical scientists invented particles, atoms, molecules, quanta which obeyed exceptionless rules in their attempt to "justify the ways of God to man."

The symbolists' particles could not be measured, converted, photographed for their effects, but they too, as we have noted, set out to reflect God's ways. In their aim they may have been only partially successful; moreover, their procedures may be applied awkwardly, sloppily, fraudulently by imitators, so that an Empson,[20] curiously reflecting Eliot's strictures on Valery in his Dante essay, may call for a return to sleek argumentative poetry. But scientific drudges with similar awkwardness and failures, may apply the procedures of the nineteenth-century scientist—while a Heisenberg, a Crick has built on them, to provide a deeper understanding of the "metre of the dictionary." The symbolists have taught us one of the features of language, one of the ways in which we "shade the patch of words left by the dead" to understand our surroundings. Besides attempting to understand their procedures, we can best express our gratitude by exploring others.

[20] William Empson's essay "Argufying in Poetry" has been widely commented on, as in letters on the version printed in the *Listener* of August 22, 1963, pp. 277–278. The following quotation may indicate that Empson does not object to symbolist poetry:

> The best poems written in English during this century are symbolist, and they are very good. But it has gone on long enough; poets are now finding the rules an obstacle, all the more because literary theorists commonly talk as if no other kind of poetry is possible but symbolist poetry.

What troubles Empson is the degeneration that often seems to follow important movements. Eliot began his celebrated essay on Dante with a critique on Verlaine's statement opposing "philosophical" poetry.

VINEGAR AND WATER

Allegory and Symbolism in the German Novelle
between Keller and Bergengruen

by
HENRY H. H. REMAK
Indiana University

VINEGAR AND WATER

Allegory and Symbolism in the German Novelle *between Keller and Bergengruen*

"I CANNOT FEEL satisfied with a literary criticism which substitutes for the conception of the writer as 'man speaking to men,' the conception of the writer as an imagination weaving symbolic patterns to be teased out by the intellect . . ." Nowadays we tend to "find significance in what the work suggests rather than what it says"; we "direct our imagination towards types and figures rather than towards their actualization."[1]

"We have, not without some ridiculous excess, pinnacled the effigy of Coleridge over the intense inane where supreme critics breathe the incense burnt in our temples."[2]

"A work of art is not just an abstruse message hidden in code. By indulging our trade in the seclusion of university seminars and almost never encountering writers, we have forgotten how fallible, how pressed by time and greed and love, how eccentric and fanciful and disorderly, how tempted by plagiarism and mystification, how unlike engineers striving for symbolic structure and functional imagery inspired writers can be."[3]

---

[1] Helen Gardner, *The Limits of Literary Criticism* (London: Oxford University Press, 1956), p. 39. My attention to this quotation was called by Henri Peyre, "Seventy-Five Years of Comparative Literature: A Backward and a Forward Glance," *Yearbook of Comparative and General Literature,* VIII (1959), 24–25.

[2] Peyre, "Seventy-Five Years of Comparative Literature," *Yearbook of . . . Literature,* p. 20.

[3] *Ibid.,* p. 25.

"Criticism is a secondary activity and should avow it. It does not have to substitute its own intellectual subtlety for the lack of it in the creator."[4]

By this time the reader may feel like A. J. Liebling, who, writing in the favorite learned periodical of American scholars, *The New Yorker,* talks about inviting his favorite aunt for dinner only to be stuck by her hatpin. Or, to come closer to home, like a big-hearted Texan pressing a black-widow spider to his bosom. But I have taken precautions. I have barricaded myself behind quotations from two very respectable people, one of whom, for increased protection, is an English lady. To add an indubitably American touch to this cosmopolitan phalanx, I need only refer to a recent explosion, "Metaphor: A Little Plain Speaking on a Weary Subject," by one of the most irritating and, I think, invigorating gadflies operating from an English Department in this country, Morse Peckham, who has assailed "the most common position to-day, the position that carries with it the richest critical and academic status and self-approval," namely that "poetry is a means of discovering a 'truth' which is accessible to no other way of thinking, and that the technique of such thinking is metaphor."[5] You should not miss his more serious than hilarious discussion of Monroe Beardsley's splendid metaphor, the chocolate kilowatt.

What is needed, I think, in the study of symbolism today is less subtlety and more sanity, more discrimination and less *cultismo,* more plain speaking and less mystification, more communication and fewer monologues within what John Livingston Lowes has called our "own solemn troops and sweet societies."[6] Let us make a modest effort to make sure, at least, that the other fellow knows what we are trying to say, an undertaking fraught, to be sure, with the danger of giving him the opportunity of discovering whether we are right or wrong.

I have felt the urge to do a little plain speaking myself at the outset of my disquisition in order not to appear as sailing wrapped from top to bottom in the flag of symbolism, an attire in which I would feel

---

[4] *Ibid.*

[5] In *Connotation,* I (Winter, 1962), 29.

[6] *The Road to Xanadu* (New York: Vintage, 1959), p. vii.

uncomfortable. I want to confess that the metaphorical, the allegorical, the symbolistic approaches to literature are, to me, only one,
two, or three ways of getting at what matters in a literary work, and
that I bear no grudge against the psychological, the ideological, the
sociological, yes, even the biographical approach, where the nature
of the work justifies their use. I agree with Georg Christoph Lichtenberg and Hugo von Hofmannsthal that "the whole man must move
together," not just aesthetic man.[7] The best defense for the symbolistic approach would be, and, I think, *is,* that it is most appropriate to *the whole man.*

Nor, once we have decided that metaphor, allegory, or symbol
hold the key or one of the keys to a work, should we fall prey to
upgrading the obvious. It is obvious that Werther will indulge in
metaphors other than those used by Lotte or Albert (and, let it be
said *en passant,* the fact that neither Lotte's nor Albert's metaphors
are as numerous or as rich as Werther's—to tell the truth, they tend
to be trite[8]—does not detract one whit from Lotte's and Albert's significance in the story). It is obvious that Faust will speak a language
different from that of Mephistopheles, Settembrini from that of
Naphta. Secondly, let us be resolutely *critical* in our review of image
patterns. Even the greatest writers will sometimes resort to hack-
neyed, misplaced, or excessive allegories, to ill-digested symbolism,
or greenhouse metaphors. It almost takes courage these days, certainly on the part of a Germanist, to assert that Goethe, yes, Goethe
himself, allegorized portions of *Faust II* to a tedious death and that
nine out of ten paladins of their excellence would be less than
charitable with them if they were not hallowed by Goethe's name.
Neither Goethe nor Hauptmann nor Thomas Mann has wholly
escaped the fatal German error of equating *Prosaliteratur* with
Bildung, the *Symbol* with the stillborn *Bildungssymbol.* It almost

[7] Lichtenberg, *Gedankenbücher,* ed. Franz H. Mautner (Frankfurt and
Hamburg: S. Fischer, 1963), p. 47. Hofmannsthal, "Die Briefe des Zurück-
gekehrten," in *Prosa II* (Frankfurt: S. Fischer, 1951), p. 325 ("The whole
man must move at once").

[8] I owe this information to an oral communication of Frank G. Ryder,
expanding on his "Season, Day, and Hour: Time as Metaphor in Goethe's
Werther," Journal of English and Germanic Philology, LXIII, No. 3 (July,
1964), 389–407.

takes courage, and exposes one to the suspicion of being low-powered, to wonder aloud what the *artistic* worth is of some of the most dazzling exhibitions of learning in symbolic garb by Thomas Mann;[9] it almost takes courage to ask where the point of diminishing returns in "imagistic" writing is reached in Proust or in Joyce or in Faulkner. It is—to end with a positive contention rather than a critical note likely to be misunderstood as gratuitous impertinence—it is the unique combination of a highly economical, deceptively concrete, yet bottomless (and very personal) symbolism, on the one hand, and an immaculate, puritan, miserly control of language, a combination of depth and leanness, of abyss and discipline, that makes of Kafka *the* towering novelistic figure of our time.

If I address myself to allegory and symbolism in certain German *Novellen* today, the preceding caveats notwithstanding, it is because symbolism is, I feel, particularly indigenous to this genre, and because this genre in which German literature of the nineteenth century and, occasionally, the twentieth century has reached the level of world literature is most inadequately known among devotees of other literatures and, indeed, among those of comparative and world literature.

Before coming to grips with particular *Novellen* I must define my terms. In an epoch when the preoccupation with metaphor, allegory, and symbol has become the badge of the "establishment," the ticket to the intellectual country club, there has been a striking dearth of intelligible definitions. I do not claim to give you a universally acceptable definition; indeed, I feel quite incapable of providing it. All I can hope to do is to give you a clear understanding of what my own definition is. I feel quite justified in choosing from the various possibilities those most suited to my particular task, to the tradition, time, authors, and subjects I am talking about. I do not postulate—far from it—that metaphor, allegory, and symbol have meant or must always mean what I take them to mean in my context.

[9] What Robert Champigny says about myth applies equally to the symbol: "A myth is anti-poetic in so far as it imposes an elaborate semantic structure" ("The *Swan* and the Question of Pure Poetry," *L'Esprit Créateur*, I [Fall, 1961], p. 148). J. C. Middleton persuasively argues the same in the latter portion of his contribution to this volume.

I consider metaphor, allegory, and symbol to be three related but distinct terms. Metaphor I deem to be the analogy of apparently disparate empirical phenomena, the linguistic concatenation of two or more observable things or events belonging to different areas of human activity and experience. A metaphor, whether simple or compound, normally starts with and ends in concrete manifestations of human endeavor.

For purposes of this investigation, allegory is the conscious stylistic disguise of one thing as another, usually the substitution of a person, an image, or an event for a concept; the intentional, rational conversion of a specific abstraction into a specific concretion. Allegory, like metaphor, is no more and no less than a manner of speaking.

The symbol, in my context, is a concrete object or, more rarely, a living being, organic part of the story, which suggests, however, one or more abstract, invisible elements or ideas giving the story a broader, more universal dimension—a *Hintergründigkeit*—whether these rapports were intended by the poet or not.

The symbol is *capable of* linking up the general with the specific, the universal with the temporal, the eternal with the accidental, the infinite with the finite, the (in philosophical terms) realistic with the nominalistic.[10] A successful, that is poetic, symbol will *intimate* this nexus through context; it will not articulate it, for "it is the essence of poetry to be ambiguous."[11] "When the soul *speaks,* alas, the *soul* speaks no longer."[12]

The metaphor, then, states a specific though unexpected relationship explicitly: $x = y$; the allegory indicates a specific relationship implicitly: $x (= y)$; the symbol implies an unspecified range of relationships: $x = (a + b + c \ldots)$. The metaphor remains on the

[10] We refer here to Professor Jaszi's deeply probing analysis of "Dauer im Wechsel," "Idee und Erscheinung," etc., elsewhere in this volume. See also Fritz Martini, "Die deutsche Novelle im 'bürgerlichen Realismus'," *Wirkendes Wort* X, No. 5 (1960), p. 267, and Walter Silz, "Geschichte, Theorie und Kunst der deutschen Novelle," *Der Deutschunterricht,* XI, No. 5 (1959), pp. 88, 91.

[11] Andrew Jaszi on p. 78 of this volume.

[12] "*Spricht* die Seele, so spricht, ach! schon die *Seele* nicht mehr" (Schiller, "Sprache," in *Votivtafeln,* Werke [Munich: Knaur, 1959], I, 200). I owe this reference to the kindness of Professor Friedrich Wilhelm Wodtke, participant in the colloquium.

same, usually pragmatic level; the allegory proceeds, in the intention of the author, from the abstract to the concrete, obliging the reader to retrace the author's steps inversely to get at its meaning; the symbol tends to be born as a particular concretion which the reader may develop and create into an abstraction or abstractions, going in the same direction, most likely, as the author did.[13]

Nature and purpose alone of these three poetic elements do not permit us to pronounce judgment on them in the hierarchy of poetic values. It is their utilization in a particular work that is decisive. Yet they possess varying ranges of poetic usefulness. Of the three, the allegory is likely to be the least rewarding to the modern author and reader. It may be ingeniously elaborated or subtly camouflaged, it may test the detective flair of the reader, but it may be little more than a show of erudition on the part of the author, an exercise of learned virtuosity, a test of the reader's *Belesenheit*. In practical use allegory, at least in the German *Novelle*, tends to be artificial, static, and trivial. The metaphor is more rewarding because it shows the creative power of the poet explicitly (or reveals its weakness), because it does not hide behind a façade of secretiveness, and because, due to the unexpectedness of linking elements and areas hitherto thought to be unrelated, it creates in the reader the desire to follow up, on his own, this new relationship. The symbol seems the most productive of the three because it does most toward making the thoughtful and sensitive reader a cocreator; it is the most dynamic of the three.[14] It thus imposes a much greater obligation on author and reader; a trite symbol is a greater crime than a trite metaphor or a trite allegory, and an undiscriminating interpretation of a symbol is a

---

[13] Alfred Zastrau, thus, is mistaken when he states that allegory in Sulzer's definition (". . . represents abstract concepts, through the senses, to perceptive cognition" [daß sie abgezogene (abstrakte) Vorstellungen dem (*sic!*) anschauenden Erkenntnis sinnlich darstellt"]) cannot be differentiated from symbol (*Goethe-Handbuch,* 2nd. edition, [Stuttgart: Metzler, n.d.], p. 136).

[14] I am encouraged to find, after the delivery of this paper, that Blake's understanding of poetry, as interpreted by Northrop Frye, tends in the same direction: "He . . . defends the practice of not being too explicit on the ground that it 'rouses the faculties to act.' . . . He expected the critic's response to be also a creative one . . . His aim is . . . to transfer to others the imaginative habit and energy of his mind" ("The Road to Excess," in *Myth and Symbol* [Lincoln: The University of Nebraska Press, 1963], pp. 3–4).

graver misdeed than an undiscriminating interpretation of an allegory or a metaphor.

Allow me to repeat: neither the inherent handicaps of the allegory
nor the inherent greater promise of the metaphor and the symbol are
factors decisive enough to block the achievement of a great allegorist
or ensure the success of a mediocre poet or symbolist. I am well aware
and appreciative of the vitality and power of metamorphosis of the
allegory as proved, for example, on the contemporary stage. I am
well aware that the most significant symbolism, though intellectually
rich, *may* be artistically poor. Nevertheless, empirically speaking, my
context, the German *Novelle* in the period investigated, justifies
qualitative differentiation in the literary potentiality of allegory and
symbol.

Being already out on a limb, I might just as well go out a little
farther yet and ask whether we can make some sort of prediction—
based on hindsight—on the relative merits of intentional vs. un-
intentional symbolism. Here it might pay to consult the poets themselves. Browning, without exactly recommending the intentional
approach, certainly does not rule it out:

> "But Art—wherein man nowise speaks to men,
> Only to mankind—Art may tell a truth
> Obliquely, do the thing shall breed the thought,
> Nor wrong the thought, missing the mediate word.
> So may you paint your picture, twice show truth,
> Beyond mere imagery on the wall—
> So, note by note, bring music from your mind,
> So write a book shall mean beyond the facts,
> Suffice the eye and save the soul besides."[15]

Nor does Goethe, and yet his constitution seems to point strongly
to the nonintentional approach; to him, symbolic representation, as
the core of poetry, "articulates something particular without thinking
of the general or pointing to it. Whoever absorbs this particularity
in its vitality receives concurrently the general, without realizing it,

[15] *The Ring and the Book* (Boston: Houghton, Mifflin and Company, 1895).
My attention was first called to this quotation by J. L. Salvan in his article
on symbolism in the *Dictionary of World Literature* (New York: Philosophical
Library, 1943), p. 567.

or realizing it but later on. . . .[16] Everything that happens is symbol, and in representing itself perfectly it points to the rest."[17] This definition is eminently applicable to the best tradition of the German *Novelle*. The *Novelle* takes a unique occurrence, disciplines it but does not adulterate it, an occurrence in which the particulars are perfectly viable in themselves, are not strained or stretched to represent the general, but provide food for thought tending toward the general, Goethe's "quiet enticement to meditate further."[18]

Only recently Walther Killy, in his book with the provocative title: *German Schmaltz (Deutscher Kitsch*[19]) did nothing but rephrase Goethe's definition in distinguishing between what he calls "pseudosymbolism," an obtrusive device contrived by the writer and dependent upon explicatory pointers, and genuine symbolism, which is a component of what happens, part of the matrix of the story—in short, something that makes sense in itself.

I would thus venture to say that the symbols more likely, in the words of Browning, to "suffice the eye" as well as "save the soul," to "twice show truth," are the ones whose range and depth are imperfectly realized by their vessel, the author, elementary rapports welling up in the poet, demonstrating their basic nature through the very unconsciousness of their eruption, intuited rather than worked out.[20]

---

[16] ". . . die Natur der Poesie . . . spricht ein Besonderes aus, ohne ans Allgemeine zu denken oder darauf hinzuweisen. Wer nun dieses Besondere lebendig faßt, erhält zugleich das Allgemeine mit, ohne es gewahr zu werden, oder erst spät" (Goethe, *Maximen und Reflexionen*, Hamburger Ausgabe, 14 vols. [Hamburg: Christian Wegner, 1960], XII, 471').

[17] "Alles, was geschieht, ist Symbol, und, indem es vollkommen sich selbst darstellt, deutet es auf das Übrige" (Letter to Carl Ernst Schubarth dated April 2, 1818, *Goethe-Briefe,* ed. Philipp Stein [Berlin: Otto Elsner, 1905], VII, 168).

[18] ". . . stillen Reiz, weiter nachzudenken" (*Unterhaltungen deutscher Ausgewanderten,* Hamburger Ausgabe, VI, 167.) Cf. Benno von Wiese's sane distinctions between allegory and symbol, based on Goethe's theory (alas, not always practice), in his "Bild-Symbole in der deutschen Novelle," *Publications of the English Goethe Society*, New Series, XXIV (1955), 132–133.

[19] Walther Killy, *Deutscher Kitsch* (Göttingen: Vandenhoeck and Ruprecht, 1962), p. 21.

[20] J. C. Middleton characterizes this kind of symbolism as "open-ended" and rightly warns against the frequent assumption that the poet who "makes

Let us try to test and illustrate these generalities through specifics. We choose as our main exhibits three works by three writers contemporary with each other, all three considered first-rate: *The Tempting of Pescara (Die Versuchung des Pescara)*, by Conrad Ferdinand Meyer (1887), *Romeo and Juliet in the Village (Romeo und Julia auf dem Dorfe)*, by Gottfried Keller (1856), and *The Rider of the White Horse (Der Schimmelreiter)*, by Theodor Storm (1888)—authors, incidentally, practically unknown to the Western World outside German-speaking areas, classics who have not even reached first base on their way toward world literature.

These stories are quite unlike each other: Meyer unfolds, against a flamboyant cinquecento tapestry, the story of a general tempted to betray the emperor; Keller describes the bourgeois decline of two peasants and the gaily and sadly beautiful love of their children ending in their deaths; Storm relates the superhuman (in more ways than one) struggle of a lone giant of a dike-reeve against outside chaos (the sea) and a stubborn, obstructionist society. The unlikeness of the stories is irrelevant here, since we are inquiring into the quality of allegorism and symbolism, not their historical or sociological appropriateness.

Meyer's *Novelle* is not five sentences old when he calls our attention to a fresco opposing a Bacchic feast to the feeding in the desert, which itself contrasts "a small and hardly visible" Christ in the background to a merry company of Lombardian reapers in the foreground.[21] This is a visual reference to the mixture of the worldly and the divine in the story, a graphic representation of the disproportionateness between the dominating worldly and the minuscule divine and Christian elements, even in the Pope himself. But this is not all yet. The happy reapers are there for a purpose. After they have been specifically connected and restricted to a happy reaping episode in the life of Pescara and his wife,[22] and further limited by Pescara to

---

meaning" is expected to "know it" (p. 103 of this volume). "The Making of meaning does involve a kind of unknowing" (*ibid.,* p. 104).

[21] Conrad Ferdinand Meyer, *Sämtliche Werke* (Munich: Droemer, 1953), p. 590.

[22] *Ibid.,* p. 654.

an allegory of death,[23] the last sentence of the *Novelle* describes Pescara, just dead, as resembling "a young, gaunt reaper, exhausted by the harvest and sleeping on his sheaf."[24] In the German original, thanks to a participial construction, "reaper" is the last word in the story, which thus begins and ends with this simile. If you bother to work out the equation, it refers not just clearly, but obviously, to the proximity of life and death, of the worldly and the religious—the merry and the grim reaper. If you don't work it out, the episodes make little sense at all; they are extraneous to the story.

Without respite, the next sentence on the first page of the *Novelle* refers us to a detail of this fresco, a flirting girl who allows a youth to embrace her and to shove a roasted fish between her "dazzling shining teeth."[25] The fish, in this context, is a further visual reference to the juxtaposition of *ecclesia* and *la dolce vita*.

Additional pictorial reinforcement comes in this chapter: another painting, this time of Pescara himself playing chess with his wife, Victoria Colonna. She fixates him with a searching, interrogative glance, while touching the queen with hesitant fingers; he, a "warrior of earnest and toilsome features, hides a smile in the severely drooping corner of his mouth."[26] The picture will be explained by the subsequent plot: Pescara's wife, tempted by the possible reward of an Italian queenship (for herself) if she can talk her husband into treason, yet slowed down by her own compunctions, wonders (like everybody else in the story) what he will do next; the grave features of the general and his drooping mouth indicate his fatal injury, as yet unknown to his wife, which makes a mockery of her ambitious attempt. Hence his smile.

To make sure *we* understand, Meyer sees to it that at the very end of this chapter the conveniently summoned moon casts its beams precisely on this chess-game painting: "What will you do, Pescara? —He was pale like death, with a smile in the corners of his mouth."[27]

The preceding examples (with one exception) all have this in

---

[23] *Ibid.*, p. 664.
[24] *Ibid.*, p. 680.
[25] *Ibid.*, p. 590.
[26] *Ibid.*, p. 596.
[27] *Ibid.*, p. 606.

common: they are extraneous elements that would have no relevance, no place in the story except as consciously introduced illustrations with a specific, limited meaning yielded by hindsight: x (= y). Bacchus and reapers represent the joy of life, Christ and (as it will turn out) again the reapers, the *memento mori*. The fish likewise juxtaposes the world and the spirit, life and death. The chess game again allegorizes life and death, the temptation of life and the knowledge of death.

The fact that Meyer had to resort to the awkward and repeated use, the artificial insemination of paintings illustrates the manipulated nature of this insertion; as a matter of fact, he will have to use three more allegorical paintings in the rest of the story to make his point: the painting, allegedly by Leonardo da Vinci, showing, among other things, a serpent swallowing a child[28] (an allegory of disaster, engineered by smart and treacherous "snakes," in store for the adolescent Duke of Milan); then a verbal painting from Dante's *Inferno,* showing the two "traitors," Brutus and Cassius, hanging head down, suspended from Lucifer's hands (an allegory of the wages of treason beckoning to Pescara);[29] finally, the altar painting in the convent, *Saints' Wounds* (*Heiligenwunden*), showing a mercenary thrusting his spear into Christ's body[30] (an allegory of the death-inflicting wound Pescara himself received at Pavia, responsible for a turn of his mind toward practiced Christianity).

To this we can safely add the living picture of Pescara slumbering on a seat flanked by two sphinxes and facing a fountain (death facing the flow of life, whose beginning and end are bathed in mystery).[31]

This is by no means the extent to which these motifs are used: the chess-game motif (*spielen* means both "playing" and "toying") continues throughout the story. Pescara is said to be toying with Italy like the cat with the mouse,[32] he toys also with his confidants (Bourbon and Del Guasto), Bourbon toys with Morone and the

[28] *Ibid.,* p. 638.
[29] *Ibid.,* p. 652.
[30] *Ibid.,* p. 662.
[31] *Ibid.,* p. 639.
[32] *Ibid.,* p. 617.

Duke of Milan, etc.; the whole *Novelle* could be compared to a chess game. The death motif is further illustrated, visualized, and repeated (spear wound, Pescara's self-personification as "death,"[33] the death [by treason!] of Julia,[34] the men responsible for Pescara's actual death [Bläsi] or plotted death [Moncada], the murder of Pescara's father [again Moncada], and finally the somewhat anachronistic appearance, in the last chapter, of Pescara as "Death the Strangler,"[35] who hardly harmonizes with the lyrical "Death the Reaper" in the same chapter). But pursuing each allegory and leitmotif to its legitimate end in this story would leave little else: it would merely confirm, with embarrassing fullness, the cumulative, oversaturated nature of Meyer's allegories—the very weaknesses which Killy has diagnosed as the difference between what he calls pseudo symbol and symbol.

Let there be no rejoinder that the culprit here is not only allegory but symbol, that the reaper, the fish, the snake, possessing double characteristics, must be classified as symbols. An allegory may refer to one abstraction or to a frozen contrast between two abstractions, or to one abstraction first and another one subsequently. It is univalent, regardless, not ambivalent or multivalent; it deliberately refers to one specific abstraction at *one* time.

The one symbolic exception to the previously cited gallery of allegories is, I think, Pescara's smile. This smile does not have a set value. It is subject to a range of interpretations. It is the quintessence of his pragmatic wisdom of life. In this particular situation, it seems to reflect an affectionate and amused understanding of his wife's quandary, a knowledge of the absurdity of the commotion of which he is the center, a philosophic acceptance of a tough break, a smile at the irony of fate offering him everything when he is nearing nothing, a detached view of Pescara the living by Pescara the already dead, and just a touch of bitterness (drooping mouth), all this against the "serious and severe" expression of a man loyal to others (king, friend Bourbon, wife) and to himself, repelled and yet somewhat attracted by the invitation to an allegedly patriotic treason.

---

[33] *Ibid.,* p. 637.
[34] *Ibid.,* p. 641.
[35] *Ibid.,* p. 673 ("der Würger Tod").

This is not an erudite picture whose key is available only to the educated, and too easily at that; this is a basic and yet complex human reaction; this is a symbol which is part of the main.

With this gratifying exception, the initial impression of static, univalent allegorization is confirmed in and by the rest of the story. The bilious Guiccardin prefers vinegar to oil, but deserves credit for providing me with the allegorical part of my title.[36] After he talks about the conspiracy, lightning and thunder furnish an operatic flourish, and, to add insult to injury, we are being informed that this is an omen.[37] The same lightning must serve again to dazzle and warn Victoria Colonna, who is rationalizing the treason.[38] But after her long prayer the heavens brighten.[39] The tempter, Morone, clad in a black coat, steps out from and steps back into the night.[40] As Pescara nears the fateful decision in his choice between loyalty and treason, midnight strikes from the clocktower, and once again Meyer puts the dot on the *i*: "The twelfth strike—irrevocable."[41] After Pescara's heart attack "the hanging lamp is extinguished," and with these words the chapter ends.[42] To Moncada's question about his goal, Pescara replies by dipping his hand into the brazier and opening it: "Dust and ashes."[43] As the defeated Duke of Milan enters his palace, the canopy over his throne collapses, and we are told that this is a bad omen.[44] And when, little later, the Duke of Bourbon smashes his goblet against the marble floor, this not only means but we are explicitly informed that it *does* mean that he is renouncing his claim to the Duchy of Milan.[45]

These thickly sprinkled and rather disconnected allegories are bordered by two personalized allegorizations; Italy—arbitrary,[46] fantastic, unreliable, but acting with heart as well as with head, disorganized but likeable, grotesque but human—is personalized by Morone (!), *Morone buffone;* Spain—cold, calculating, fanatic, intelligent, cruel, consistent, well-organized, born to rule but inhuman

[36] *Ibid.*, p. 597.
[37] *Ibid.*, p. 612.
[38] *Ibid.*, p. 614.
[39] *Ibid.*
[40] *Ibid.*
[41] *Ibid.*, p. 657.
[42] *Ibid.*, p. 658.
[43] *Ibid.*, p. 672.
[44] *Ibid.*, p. 673.
[45] *Ibid.*, p. 675.
[46] See Benno von Wiese, *Die deutsche Novelle von Goethe bis Kafka* (Düsseldorf: Bagel, 1956), I, 265.

—by the monkish Moncada (!). Even though these humanized
countries exhibit various characteristics, the equation remains the
same everywhere: $x = y$.

We cannot here take the time to investigate thoroughly the similes
in the *Versuchung des Pescara*. They seem about as shopworn as the
allegories discussed above. Two examples: the rumor of Pescara's
impending desertion is compared to the fountains of Italian *piazzas*:
both are equally public.[47] Aside from the relative staleness of the
comparison itself, a little thinking shows that the comparison is very
superficial. A fountain runs evenly, steadily; rumors in cities and inns
circulate with much more uncertainty, with unpredictable pauses.
The limipidity of the water is hardly a suitable simile for the opaque
substance of treason. On the same page, Italy's advances to Pescara
are described as follows: "Italy throws herself into his arms . . . he
will caress, subjugate, and discard her . . ., oh, he will play with her
like the cat with the mouse.[48] It is certainly possible to caress, con-
quer, and abandon a woman or, stretching the metaphor, even a
country; it is likewise possible to toy with someone, as the cat with
the mouse, but to have metaphor and simile mixed up in the same
exclamation is not only unnecessarily cumulative but borders on the
absurd. A mouse does not throw itself into the arms of a cat; a cat
does not have arms; a cat does not caress a mouse; a woman throw-
ing herself into someone's arms is everything but a mouse. The first
metaphor, by itself, would be quite dashing, except that Italy, the
woman, is not animated by patriotic passion only, but by all kinds
of ulterior motives in making advances to Pescara. The second, cat-
and-mouse, simile, is appropriate neither to Pescara nor to Italy.
Both juxtaposed in the same sentence are frightfully ill-matched. The
mediocrity of the imagery confirms the mediocrity of the allegory.

I am certainly not the first one to have seen these weaknesses, although even those who have detected them appear anxious to soften
the unmistakable verdict.[49] But, worse than that, even the *critical*

[47] Meyer, *Sämtliche Werke,* p. 617.
[48] *Ibid.*
[49] Benno von Wiese, while admitting weakness, nevertheless credits Meyer,
in *Pescara,* with "a high degree of novellistic ability" ("einen hohen Grad
novellistischen Könnens," *Novelle* [Stuttgart: Metzler, 1963], p. 68). H. M.
Waidson refers to *Pescara,* along with *Michael Kohlhaas: Die schwarze Spinne*

observers continue to speak of the *symbolic* power of these images.[50] As I hope to have shown, the imagery I have dealt with, excepting one instance, is allegorical, not symbolical, univalent rather than ambivalent or multivalent, static rather than dynamic, extraneous rather than intrinsic, intentional rather than organic.

This is not to say that allegorization, sparsely and deftly or humorously used, cannot be a real asset to the *Novelle*. Take Keller's delightful story, *Clothing Makes People* (*Kleider machen Leute*, 1873/4).[51] The title being what it is, clothing is bound to be involved in the imagery of the story—it is a "natural." The thimble stands for the "tailoresque" part of the hero; fur-cap, velvet-trimmed coat, and gloves for the aristocratic bearing of Wenzel Strapinski befit the dark-haired darling of fate. Note that these are functional attributes, objects that serve practical purposes while serving as specific allegories. They are used economically, and always with a sense of humor. It is true that there are places in the story where Keller accumulates whole mountains of allegories:[52] houses with allegorical names (the House of the Golden Dragon, of the Swiss Sword, of the Unicorn, of the Bird of Paradise, of Old Independence, of New Independence, of Civic Virtue A, of Civic Virtue B,[53] of "Zum Wiedersehen 1 und 2,"[54] and others, but these are affectionate take-offs on Swiss history and bourgeois virtues, and even when the sun breaks through as an allegory of Strapinski's ascending fortune[55] the humorous coloring of the situation is unmistakable.

---

and *Romeo und Julia,* as one of the "characteristic masterpieces of the nineteenth-century Novelle" (in the revised edition of E. K. Bennett's *A History of the German Novelle* [Cambridge: University Press, 1961], p. 241).

[50] Johannes Klein, *Geschichte der deutschen Novelle von Goethe bis zur Gegenwart* (Wiesbaden: Steiner, 1960), p. 48; von Wiese, *Die deutsche Novelle*, I (1956), pp. 252, 267; von Wiese, *Novelle*, p. 68.

[51] There seems to be a connection between the typifying intent of a *Novelle* and a corresponding richness in allegories: *Kleider machen Leute, Die drei gerechten Kammacher, Aquis Submersus, Der Ketzer von Soana, Der Schleier.*

[52] From here on I expand, now and then, on pointers contained in my "Theorie und Praxis der Novelle: Gottfried Keller," in *Stoffe, Formen, Strukturen* (Munich: Hueber, 1962), pp. 432–437.

[53] Gottfried Keller, *Sämtliche Werke* (Munich: Droemer, 1953, 2 vols.), I, 823.

[54] *Ibid.,* p. 818.

[55] *Ibid.,* p. 812.

We recently proposed the hypothesis that the looser the silhouette of the *Novelle,* represented by the unified occurrence of *one event* (the *eine Begebenheit* of Goethe's famous definition of the *Novelle*[56]), the greater the necessity for the author to save the concentration indispensable to the *Novelle* by other means.[57] Among the most effective of these means are image-"falcons" ("Bild-Falken"), object-symbols (*Dingsymbole*) and musical "falcons" (*Leitmotive*). We further suggested, and venture to broaden this into a more general hypothesis at this time, that when the silhouette of the action is still relatively unified and striking but needs some reinforcement through images, the use of allegory may be adequate to meet this purpose (witness *Kleider machen Leute*) ; but when the *Novelle* threatens to burst its classic boundaries (as it does in the *Versuchung des Pescara*) to the extent of jeopardizing the *Gestalt* of the genre as such, the accumulation of allegories—Meyer's remedy—will not do. On the contrary, allegorical proliferation, as in the *Versuchung,* may have the effect of scattering attention in all directions, of offering too many disconnected and univalent images—of further weakening the structure of the *Novelle.* A quantitative corrective is likely to prove impotent. A qualitative compensation is much more likely to do the job, and that is the upgrading of the allegory to a symbol—in the *Novelle,* normally an object-symbol. Being more pervasive, more encompassing, more flexible, it can link a whole story through no more than one or two principal symbols; being multivalent, it is better suited to hold the *Novelle* together than univalent allegory. It is true that the appropriateness and the quality of the symbol then become much more decisive for the story than the relevance and persuasiveness of one of several or many allegories. This would fit into the high degree of workmanship, of artistic responsibility that characterizes the best products of the German *Novelle.* At the same time, as soon as conscious efforts to create symbols are involved, the symbol may become a rational construct lacking in life, in veracity, which is precisely what

[56] Goethe to Eckermann, January 25, 1827: "Was ist eine Novelle anders als eine sich ereignete unerhörte Begebenheit" (*Eckermanns Gespräche mit Goethe,* ed. Ernst Merian-Genast [Basel: Birkhäuser, 1945], I, 210).

[57] See my "Theorie und Praxis der Novelle: Gottfried Keller," *Stoffe, Formen, Strukturen,* p. 433.

will happen to certain well-known examples of the genre by Gerhart Hauptmann, Emil Strauss, and Werner Bergengruen. In the finest *Novellen*, symbols, though subject to rational polishing, must be functional and, as it were, instinctive by birth.

For possible illustrations of this hypothesis let us look at what are probably the best two German *Novellen* of the second half of the nineteenth century, Keller's *Romeo and Juliet in the Village* (*Romeo und Julia auf dem Dorfe*) and Theodor Storm's *Rider of the White Horse* (*Der Schimmelreiter*).

Romeo und Julia is not devoid of allegory, and this allegory is not necessarily bad. To be sure, when the two peasants, locked in a fatal struggle that paralyzes them as surely as two drowning persons clasping each other, meet on a "narrow, tottering bridge," under lightning and thunder, there is too direct a connection, I am afraid, between the "rumbling rancor" of the thunder and of the protagonists, the "heavy raindrops" and their tears; the setting of the scene, not the scene itself, has something Hollywoodish.[58] Compare it to the deluge at the conclusion of the *Schimmelreiter*: what is a theatrical and dispensable stagesetting in Keller becomes, in Storm, a necessary and organic, cataclysmic showdown between the forces of evil and good, chaos and civilization, the sea and man—Armageddon.

But other allegories in *Romeo und Julia* and the *Schimmelreiter* are quite effective. Colors have a powerful impact in *Romeo und Julia*: the redness of the lonely poppy in the abandoned field where the children play[59] and later on, amidst "innumerable poppies," love each other in earnest,[60] the cherry-redness of the skirt of one of the "gypsies,"[61] the sturdy, unpruned rose bushes developing on their own around their place of amusement,[62] the comparison of Vrenchen to a purple rose[63] or a red carnation,[64] the "necklace and belt of small red berries" of the five-year-old girl,[65] intensified—similar to the

[58] Keller, *Sämtliche Werke*, I, 668–670. Here I cannot be quite as forbearing as Walter Silz in his *Realism and Reality: Studies in the German Novelle of Poetic Realism* (Chapel Hill: University of North Carolina Press, 1956), p. 87.

[59] Keller, *Sämtliche Werke*, I, 654, 655.

[60] *Ibid.*, pp. 675, 677.

[61] *Ibid.*, p. 698.   [63] *Ibid.*, p. 699.   [65] *Ibid.*, p. 654.

[62] *Ibid.*, p. 697.   [64] *Ibid.*, p. 693.

poppy motif above—to a "sextuple necklace of rowan-berries" of another one of these "bohemians,"[66]—and I have not exhausted the instances—all of these stand for one and the same thing: the "surging blood"[67] of the two lovers, particularly of Vrenchen, their desire for union. At first reading this allegory is functional and unobtrusive, at second and third readings one detects its (still functional) richness, and at tenth reading one wishes there were a little less of it. But who reads a work ten times except a professor? Is it fair to judge a *Novelle* not written for petulant scholars but for a non-professional, yet sensitive and intelligent, audience, by our highly specialized, academic standards alone? Be that as it may—and I am asking a question which is not a rhetorical one—the "red" allegory in *Romeo und Julia* is effective because, though univalent, it is richly suggestive, yet simple and common.

Nevertheless, the story could quite conceivably have proceeded without it; the allegory is, no matter how warm and rich, an added touch. It reminds one of the ash tree ("Ebereschel") in the *Schimmelreiter* which stands, in lone grandeur, by the side of the old dikegrave's house, "visible from afar";[68] the tree vaults over the handshake, signifying, for all intents and purposes, the engagement of Elke, only child of the old dikegrave, and Hauke, the dikegrave-to-be; it rustles over the married but childless Elke;[69] beneath it the eerie white horse, one of the key symbols of the story, makes his first appearance;[70] from the tree Hauke takes his last departure, Elke catches the last glance of her husband.[71] The ash tree is, clearly, allegorical; it represents the continuity of the Volkerts, then of the Haien family, the dike-reeve dynasty. It occurs at least nine times in this role. Before Hauke's final departure—appropriately, perhaps too appropriately —"the old ash-tree creaks, as if it were to burst asunder."[72] The ash tree does not clash with the North Sea landscape; it is rare but not foreign; it represents a basic organism; it is picturesque, it is visu-

---

[66] *Ibid.*, p. 698.

[67] *Ibid.*, pp. 700, 703. See also Ernst Feise, "Kellers *Romeo und Julia* und Stifters *Brigitta*: Aufbau und Gehalt," in *Xenion: Themes, Forms, and Ideas in German Literature* (Baltimore: The Johns Hopkins Press, 1950), p. 160.

[68] Theodor Storm, *Werke* (Munich: Droemer, 1953), p. 902.

[69] *Ibid.*, p. 926.   [71] *Ibid.*, p. 967.

[70] *Ibid.*, p. 935.   [72] *Ibid.*

ally impressive. But it is nevertheless quite unusual, the highest tree in the village, a distinction perhaps too obvious; only survivor of three ash trees planted by Elke's great-grandfather; it is, let us admit it, a stage prop with a very specific assignment, nicely, cleverly reinforced throughout the story; it is expendable. In comparison, the heap of stones separating the fields of Manz and Marti in *Romeo und Julia* is structural, endemic;[73] it would roughly correspond to the dike in the *Schimmelreiter*.

What images in these two stories *are* centripetal, elementary symbols?[74] In *Romeo und Julia,* field and river, functional manifestations of two of the four traditional elements of life: earth and water. The well-tilled soil is the very foundation of rural existence, the staff of life for the two peasants, Manz and Marti, the nutrient of civilization. It stands for more than the prosperity of its owners; it guarantees the continuity of the society which seems as unshakeable as the creases of the knee-breeches of those tilling this good earth.[75] But there is untilled earth between the tilled areas of earth, a wild plot of land covered with weeds and stones, a symbol of neglect and disorder, and, as it turns out, of intentional or, at least, tolerated injustice to its déclassé owner. The growth of the stone wall separating the once good neighbors becomes, as it is these days in Berlin, the visible token of the inhumanity of man toward man, the separation of families and lovers, the grotesque sundering of what belongs together; it is, alas, nothing but the monumental reflection of the rigid disposition of the bearers of the breeches which Keller describes as "chiseled in stone"[76] on the first page of his *Novelle.*

This, then, is already a polar symbolism reaching to the roots of mankind's existence and troubles. But Keller goes it one better yet;

[73] Udo Kultermann includes in his excellent analysis of "Bildformen in Kellers Novelle *Romeo und Julia auf dem Dorfe*" (*Der Deutschunterricht,* VIII, No. 3 [1956], 86–100) a discussion of stone symbolism.

[74] See Susanne K. Langer's observations on "charged" symbols, basic phenomena, and objects (a sunset, a cross, a ship) inherently loaded with symbolic meaning (*Philosophy in a New Key* [New York: Pelican, 1948], pp. 231–232). Reginald Phelps notes Keller's "liking for symbolism . . . of a rather simple kind" ("Keller's Technique of Composition in *Romeo und Julia auf dem Dorfe,*" *Germanic Review,* XXIV, No. 1 [1949], p. 42).

[75] Keller, *Sämtliche Werke,* p. 651.

[76] *Ibid.*

for this negative symbol, trapped and staring out from in between
two positive, life-giving symbols, becomes, in turn, the source of the
positive potentialities of disorder. Again, as early as the first page,
Keller tells us that "a world of tiny winged creatures hummed undis-
turbed above" this "fallow waste," enjoying the opportunities of ir-
regularity.[77] The earth has caught up with the stones, has grown over
them in magic profusion, equilibrium is being restored, bright red
poppies shoot out of the desert—allegories, if you wish, blossom on
symbols, life and love arise from stone. For it is on this very forsaken
field that Sali and Vrenchen find each other, first at the ages of seven
and five, in playful love; it is on the top of the stony crest that they
see each other, once a year, during the period of their enforced separation; it is there that they spend their first happy day together as
adolescents before the final break between their parents; it is there
that they first kiss each other; it is along this crest that they walk
"quietly, happily and calmly"[78] like a promised couple; it is there that
the exuberant music of a "wild wedding" ceremony fades into the
distance[79] and they take the decision to marry and die without bene-
fit of clergy.[80] The soil carries them from childhood to wedding,
which equals death.

The other pole of their existence is the river. Their destiny takes
them from the land that first brings them together, separates them,
then unites them again, to the water that first separates them,[81] above
which, on a shaky bridge leading across, they seal their first, fleeting
union with "hands moist and cool from the water and the fish,"[82]
on which they celebrate their wedding night, and in which they die
as one. As indispensable to existence as to the soil, it represents the
flowing rather than the solid, the liquid and unfathomable instead of
the firm, change rather than continuity, the irretrievable and irresistible rather than the stable, the dynamic rather than the static. I
should not have said it "represents"; it *is,* or rather it *becomes.*[83] The

---

[77] *Ibid.*
[78] *Ibid.,* p. 674.
[79] *Ibid.,* p. 702.

[80] *Ibid.,* p. 703.
[81] *Ibid.,* p. 668.
[82] *Ibid.,* p. 670.

[83] Professor Jaszi's relevant comments, in the discussion following the delivery of this paper, have called my attention to the danger of backsliding into
"static" verbs ("represents"), more appropriate to allegorism, when trying to
describe the nature and power of the symbol.

water symbol here derives an ironic depth from its ambiguity: as life-giving soil here, in the shape of a contested field, gives rise to ruin and ultimately death, so life-giving water becomes the place and means of ruin (the illusory fishing expeditions of Manz, Marti, and the Seldwylers) and of death.[84] Liquid, the biological source of life, the distinct quality of the erotic and procreative, becomes the medium of a death as immaculate as its victims, cleansing them of any possible stains, a means of expiation if sin occurred. Ironically enough, self-righteous public opinion will equate this voluntary submergence only with the theft of the hay barge which has to serve the two lovers as their nuptial couch, with what Keller, sarcastically, calls "rampaging immorality" and "barbarization of passion."[85]

I submit that this is symbolism at its best. Not at its only, but at its best. Mark that the story makes perfect sense as a story, is, with very occasional lapses, natural and unforced and convincing without any symbolic interpretation at all.[86] The search into its symbolism adds implied dimensions but does not disqualify or invalidate or truncate findings that do not penetrate all these layers. This is the kind of symbolism that is not dependent upon *a* key, *a* formula, an intricate combination accessible only to the highly sophisticated mind, or perhaps invented by it, as Mr. Peyre has suggested.[87]

I insist that the most complex symbolic interpretation is not necessarily the "right" one. Complexity *may* be superficial, may mean muddled thinking, unable to separate the chaff from the wheat, waning artistic strength. Excess of symbolism and allegory is a greater offense than too little or none, for its camouflages mediocrity. The

---

[84] For pertinent observations on the water motif, see Helmut Rehder, "*Romeo und Julia auf dem Dorfe:* An Analysis," *Monatshefte,* XXXV, No. 8 (December, 1943), 422 ff. See also Feise, "Kellers *Romeo und Julia* . . . ," *Xenion,* p. 158.

[85] Keller, *Sämtliche Werke,* p. 705.

[86] "I believe that the proper and perfect symbol is the natural object, that if a man use 'symbols' he must so use them that their symbolic function does not obtrude; so that a sense, and the poetic quality of the passage, is not lost to those who do not understand the symbol as such, to whom, for instance, a hawk is a hawk" (*Literary Essays by Ezra Pound,* ed. T. S. Eliot [London: Faber and Faber, 1954], p. 9).

[87] Peyre, "Seventy-Five Years of Comparative Literature," *Yearbook of* . . . *Literature,* p. 25.

best *Novelle* is the one that does justice to the polarities and ironies of human existence without sacrificing the functional concreteness, the "truthfulness" and the limpidity of storytelling inherent in the genre.

Examined by these demanding standards, Storm's *Schimmelreiter* will be found fully comparable to Keller's *Romeo und Julia* in the organic quality of its main symbols: horse, sea, and dike. The sea, seen throughout the story from the land, is the demonic-destructive,[88] the rebellion of the elements, fate, night, death, nothingness rushing tigerlike to tear up the defense which human order, Christian civilization have thrown up against the onslaught of chaos: the dike. These constituents of existence are humanized in the dominating creatures of the story: Hauke Haien and his *Schimmel*. The acquisition of the raggety, ill-treated horse seems a Christian act, a bad bargain intentionally concluded by a compassionate man expressing thanks for the completion of his plans for a new dike. This down-in-the-dumps horse fattens up, however, into a vigorous steed that flies through the air like Odin's horse. There was more method than madness in Hauke's acquisition of an essentially sound but run-down animal. Rider and horse develop a reciprocal magnetism evolving into fusion, an elementary attraction that reinforces Hauke's own demonic instincts, becomes a living symbol of his *hybris* at war with his *ratio* as the sea rages against the dike outside him. We ask ourselves whether chaos has not planted its own seeds beneath the rational upper layer of Hauke. Will chaos, which does not only exist outside but inside, will the sea have the last laugh, after all, a "horse-laugh," as it has already come back at Elke and Hauke by "casting a curse" on their only child? For Wienke, too, exemplifies this mixture of heathen and Christian elements, a mixture which manages at once to be complex and perfectly natural, for in this Germanic territory along the North Sea the fringes remain pagan to this very day: the pagan and Christian elements are intertwined and superimposed. The pagan undertow of this coastal area would be inclined to cast Wienke off as a creature that is not viable, an underprivileged being

---

[88] The life-giving properties of water (e.g., fishing) are here dwarfed by its life-taking nature; see not only Hauke's and Elke's fate but also the death of Trine Jans' son in a shipwreck.

eligible for sacrifice like a bastard dog or a gipsy child. But father and
mother accept and love her in the spirit of Christianity as they have
saved the horse, the dog, and the sea gull. Yet the child herself has
unbreakable ties with the elementary, she belongs to another world,
she has a strange attraction to and for the demonic (Trine Jans, the
sea), she is forever accompanied by creatures which themselves are
animalic in origin but domesticated, humanized by man, hybrid
beings: sea gull and dog.

No matter how far we descend into this abyss, uncharted depths
remain. The ultimate act of the dikegrave, his voluntary jump into
the raging sea, preserves its secret, for it, too, may be interpreted as a
Christian act of contrition for his *hybris,* a last gesture of love and
loyalty to wife and daughter, already drowned, or as a more pagan
than Christian attempt to placate the sea by offering it the human
sacrifice of life which he had stubbornly withheld from it until this
time. And the sea understands, and respects the bargain: the Hauke-
Haien dike is left intact, the dike which in itself is a symbol of rational
order, of selflessness—and of pride amounting to *hybris.*

When an author has succeeded in creating, in two or three symbols, a fusion of rational and irrational, of the unique and the permanent, of action and meaning, an entity whose components make
sense as integral parts of the story, make sense also in their polar relationships, but whose interlacing, whose various combinations seem
inexhaustible though none does violence either to the story or to the
universe against which the story moves, then the author has achieved
the well-nigh impossible. Keller and Storm have done it in these
two stories that belong to world literature. They could not have done
it without the universal power of the symbol.

In *Railguard Thiel (Bahnwärter Thiel)*, by Gerhart Hauptmann
(1887), we have, perhaps, the last contemporary German *Novelle*
in which the object-symbol fulfils adequately—in this case, admir-
ably—its centripetal role, in its logical and emotional magnetism as
well as its organic imbeddedness in the story. Hauptmann has captured a symbol of technology, the railroad, and has given it universal
yet very concrete meaning. It is the monster that arises, as the tiniest
black dot, on the farthest point of the horizon, almost invisible, that
grows, first very slowly, soon with frightful speed, that descends upon

us like an envoy of chaos,[89] rattles, snorts, roars, screams toward us like a modern version of Odin's wild hunt, like a technological *Schimmelreiter*, grazes us with its wings of disaster, the apocalypse of the day of judgment. On Thiel's day of judgment, which becomes also that of Lene and of the "brat" (*der Balg*[90]), it no longer grazes us, it runs right into us, into Tobias, bouncing him and us around like a rubber ball.

The rails, it has been remarked, grasp Thiel's existence as hypnotically, as octopuslike as the animal scent of his second wife, Lene.[91] He does not really understand its meaning. The emperor who once traveled from Berlin to Breslau along the rails guarded by Thiel remains invisible to him. All he derives from passing trains, even before his son is killed by one of them, are grave injuries caused by a wine bottle casually thrown out or a piece of coal. Nevertheless, the machine is not depicted as a one-dimensional malefactor (as so frequently in German literature of the time, unless it is ignored entirely as being "unpoetic"). His service is faithful in the fullest sense of the word, for it involves not only loyalty to his appointed work, but faithfulness to his former, cleaner, more spiritual existence, "Dienst" not only to the ethos of work, of "Arbeit," the badge of nobility, as Silz has seen so well,[92] of poetic realism, but also "Minnedienst"—"Dienst an Minna," his first wife, his truly better half. The two together keep him clean. His railroad post becomes a religious sanctuary which he defends against the intrusions of his sexual partner, and when this defense collapses outwardly and Thiel half acquiesces in the invasion of the hard-working animal, his present wife, his resentment, his squashed piety are pressed into the depths of his subconscious, only to explode again, after the killing of his son by the railroad (!) train through the neglect of his second wife, as a double murder of revenge and self-cleansing. Hauptmann has given the railroad a soul, not only in the lonely guardhouse altar where Thiel worships Minna, but in the wondrous sounds which, as we all know, emanate from telegraph wires along the rails and from the rails themselves if we bend down

---

[89] von Wiese, *Die deutsche Novelle,* I, 271.
[90] Gerhart Hauptmann, *Bahnwärter Thiel* (Stuttgart: Reclam, 1962), p. 43.
[91] von Wiese, *Die deutsche Novelle,* I, p. 273.
[92] Walter Silz, *Realism and Reality,* p. 144.

and listen to them. He has bedded, finally, the sober and yet so frightfully portentous rails into the equally sober and melancholy stretches
of sand and pines of the Mark Brandenburg, whose lonely leanness
and beautiful sadness form the nutrient for direct, individualistic
communication with the divine, which crosses the tracks as a squirrel.

Since *Bahnwärter Thiel* the overwhelming complexity of contemporary life has made it just about impossible for an artist even of the
first magnitude to write a representative *Novelle* held together by a
truly comprehensive symbol. The attempts to return to the more
classic form of the *Novelle* have either been failures or only partly successful. To the failures belongs Emil Strauss' *The Veil (Der Schleier,*
1920), usually grossly overrated.

The veil, in its whiteness, lightness, softness, translucence, and
adaptability, its marital and religious connotations, is a lovely femi-
nine symbol, but scarcely appropriate to the twentieth century. Representing, as it here does, the early matrimonial happiness of a noble
couple, a wife's silent exhortation of an errant husband and, at the
same time, her merciful[93] tribute to a second honeymoonlike, quasi-
marital happiness of her husband with his mistress, it is a grand, beautiful, and symbolic gesture totally incredible, alas, stylized, purified
so as to make complete constructs of these timelessly impossible and
oh so wonderfully generous people.

Although Bergengruen's *Three Falcons (Die drei Falken,* 1937)
is better literature than the *Schleier,* the falcon symbol, reminiscent
of Boccaccio, is an elegant failure. The boldness, dignity, and *noblesse*
of the falcons, their self-restraint and voluntary service, so to speak,
superimposed on their love of liberty, are impressive but too remote
from the twentieth century and probably at home in none. They are
centripetal in the story, but marginal in their existential application
to modern life. In order to give them more universal meaning, Bergengruen has tried to make them representative of humanity: as
there are noble and ignoble falcons, so there is selfless and selfish humanity, the latter portrayed by a silkdealer couple, a covetous young

---

[93] The veil in Brentano's *Geschichte vom braven Kasperl und dem schönen
Annerl* and in Keller's *Kleider machen Leute* also carries the connotation of
mercy. See B. A. Rowley's introduction to *Kleider machen Leute* (London:
Arnold, 1960), p. 25.

widow, and one part of Albinelli, executor of the will; the former
portrayed by the late falconer, the prior of the monastery of the Holy
Ghost, the better part of Albinelli, and of Cecco, the limping bastard,
natural son of the falconer. All these pieces fall much too neatly into
place; the *Novelle* does not spring to life.

For analogous reasons, the allegorism in Hauptmann's *Heretic of
Soana (Der Ketzer von Soana,* 1911–1917)—and here I know I go
against strongly entrenched opinion—is a failure all the more pain-
ful since it comes from a man who started out as a first-rate artist and
has much greater ambitions in this story than Bergengruen in his.
Hauptmann's would-be symbolism is to take in the Dionysian and
the Christian antitheses, though feeble attempts are made to connect
them here and there, for example, the shepherd of the Christian flock
with a real, heathen goatherd.[94] The result is, unfortunately, a
sophomoric kind of allegorism, so direct, contrived, and self-enclosed
as to be an insult to the intelligent reader, a "symbolism" all too
clearly fed by encyclopedias and reference works—a *"Bildungssym-
bolik."*[95] The he-goat (*Ziegenbock*) allegorizes the sexually aggres-
sive male, and it is hardly necessary for Hauptmann to have him
swallow the priest's breviary to indicate that eros will dispose of Christian asceticism.[96] Even less necessary is the ride on top of the goat the
author imposes on the female embodiment of eros, Agata,[79] or the
schoolmasterly comment of the goatherd to his visitor as they watch
two bucks fight: "Eros! Eros!"[98]

On top of this are piled additional sexual allegories, apparently in
the belief that intensity can be achieved by accumulation: the far-
fetched copulative allegory of a "black thunderstorm resting on the
giant dorsal rock of the Monte Generoso (!) like a huge steer resting
on a heifer, practicing with panting loins the procreative work of fer-

[94] Gerhart Hauptmann, *Der Ketzer von Soana* (Gütersloh: Bertelsmann,
1955), p. 42.

[95] There is no denying, of course, that there are fine and authentic, if somewhat monotonous, southern nature descriptions in this work of Hauptmann.

[96] Hauptmann, *Der Ketzer von Soana,* p. 62.

[97] *Ibid.,* p. 112.

[98] *Ibid.,* p. 16. This is but a striking illustration of the overemphasis on
didactic "prodesse" and the slighting of poetic "delectare" in much of German
literary prose.

tilization";[99] a further male-aggressive sexual allegory is the leitmotif of the fishing eagle circling over the same Monte Generoso, an image employed, with slight variation, when Francesco the priest shoots down like a falcon on Agata's lip,[100] there is the phallic idol, the priapus, winning over the cross, there is the sarcophagus, decorated with Dionysian scenes, in which the luscious women of Soana do their laundry, casting inviting glances at their saintly priest (triumph of life over death again, in case you don't know) ; there is the female erotic allegory of the "young apple trees,"[101] the crack in the tree bark and voluptuous lines of the mountains;[102] and, if you are difficult to please, we have for you, to top it off, the omnipresent waterfall, no doubt indicating passion, accompanying the action from beginning to end. Not one of them is necessary to the story. Each and everyone is dragged in as a stage requisite and pointed at with the index finger: "Here! Don't you see?" The sensuous balsam of Hauptmann's story has so seduced its middle-aged professorial readers, craving, like Faust, for sexual rejuvenation, that few of them have bothered to examine the pitifully conventional, ill-matched, and overdone imagery of the story.

*   *   *   *   *

We can only conjecture what the future of the symbol in the *Novelle* will be, or, in view of the atomization of our life, whether it has a future at all. Archetypal symbolism was the natural way of expression for earlier, highly structured, centripetal societies governed by recognized symbols regulating life. In any modern society seeking a return to primitivistic patterns (fascism, nazism, communism), centripetal symbols stage a forced comeback. In our western, centrifugal society (witness, for example, the declining fortunes of mass rallies and national celebrations in this country), centripetal symbols either seem no longer the organic way of expression, or when new symbols (the airplane, the "bomb," missiles) are replacing the old ones, literature has a hard time catching up with them.[103]

This centrifugal trend has been offset, to an extent, by the redis-

---

[99] *Ibid.*, p. 101.   [101] *Ibid.*, p. 141.
[100] *Ibid.*, p. 136.   [102] *Ibid.*, p. 68.
[103] See Langer, *Philosophy in a New Key*, pp. 227, 234. Cf. also Professor Brinkmann's contribution to this volume.

covery of the primitive within us, which has resulted in a flourishing archetypal symbolism in contemporary literature and criticism.

Since the symbol is a key factor in the finest achievements of the nineteenth-century *Novelle,* we must ask ourselves, in the light of this prognosis, whether the *Novelle* itself has a future in the twentieth century? It certainly does not have much of a present. It is not the obsession with violence of our present-day literature and, alas, not only literature, that threatens the *Novelle,* which has thrived on violence, nor the absurdity of existence which we find, from one of the earliest and still the finest teller of *Novellen,* Heinrich von Kleist, via Keller's *Die drei gerechten Kammacher* to Hauptmann's *Bahnwärter Thiel.* But can the classic economy of form of the *Novelle,* its lean clarity, its taut explosiveness—still respected and carried, as a matter of fact, to uncanny perfection by Kafka—can it survive the wild experimentation in language (not thought) of today and tomorrow, can the symbol as a unifying factor survive the reckless centrifugal sprinkling about of assorted symbols so fashionable in today's literature, art, and cinema? Only time can tell.

Hofmannsthal's best novelistic efforts (*Bassompierre, Reitergeschichte*) and Thomas Mann's *Der kleine Herr Friedemann, Tristan, Der Tod in Venedig, Mario und der Zauberer*) seem to rely less on central symbolism than on a mixture of object-symbolism, allegories (often ironic), leitmotif, and unity of mood. Thomas Mann's symbolism is highly conscious, cerebrally worked out, "expendable," allegoric, in short. But not only—certainly in *Tristan* and especially in *Der Tod in Venedig*—is it handled with such exquisite artistic finesse that it creates the poetic texture of his stories, not only does the combination of intellectual "raffinement" and literary tact produce an *aesthetic* pleasure, but it often resides in a twilight zone between allegory and symbol in which Mann's sophistication makes sport of professorial endeavors to establish viable theoretical distinctions. Thus, in *Der Tod in Venedig,* the various "Dance of Death" figures are clearly allegorical, but the nature of death itself, strictly within the context of the story—beauty and decomposition, liberation and humiliation, truth and impudence, authenticity and degradation, self-fulfilment and self-abandonment, etc.—is so complex and "open-ended" that the allegory ends up as a symbol. We cannot venture into this hybrid realm within the frame of this paper.[104]

We can perhaps anticipate, concurrently with the decline of the symbol, a dramatic reintensification of the story, of the action, compensating the *Novelle* for the tautness lost with the vanishing symbol. Such a shift, a very hypothetical one at this moment, would reverse the trend of the last seventy-five years, in which the symbol has tended to fill the vacuum left by the decline of sharply profiled action formerly guaranteeing some sort of unity to the *Novelle*.

There is another possibility. A dominant image maintains, perhaps fortifies, its central role, but, reflecting the brokenness of contemporary life, evolves from the relative firmness of the "symbol" to the intentional vagueness of a "signal," a "token." In Kafka's *Country Doctor* (*Ein Landarzt*, 1918), the horses—functional, central, existential, and artistically convincing—seem to run the gamut from the (illusion of the) trusty helpers of man to the envoys of a demonic supreme power unknown to us, unfathomable, irresistible, apparently illogical, working toward ends, if any, we can never know, and with consequences overwhelmingly negative. Musil's *Blackbird* (*Die Amsel*, 1928) brings a liberating beckon from afar (childhood? death? the supernatural? God?).[105]

In the meantime all we can do is to look back at the golden age of the German *Novelle*, the nineteenth century, from Kleist to Hofmannsthal, and conclude that the few best *Novellen* are those with the most elementary symbolism, be it earth or water, dike or sea, horses or rails, and that straight allegories tend to leave a sour taste in our mouths, like C. F. Meyer's vinegar. Vinegar is good as flavoring, but one cannot drink it straight. Humorous and ironic allegories,

[104] For a point of departure, see von Wiese's "Bild-Symbole," *Publications of the English Goethe Society*, p. 157, and his analysis of "Der Tod in Venedig" in *Die deutsche Novelle*, I (1956), particularly pages 310–324. The synopsis of Haskell M. Block's "Allegory and Symbol: A Reappraisal," *Actes du IIIe Congrès de l'Association Internationale de Littérature Comparée* (['s-Gravenhage: Mouton, 1962], p. 346) points to a detached, comprehensive survey of the distinction and interaction between allegory and symbol in western scholarship since the eighteenth century.

[105] Benno von Wiese, *Die deutsche Novelle*, II, 299–318.

from Keller's thimble to Mann's proper names, can complement the earnestness of symbolism; the specific-ironic can season the pervasive-problematic, entertainment and wit can humanize the metaphysical, to give the best *Novellen* that flavor of the unique, unobtrusively and yet compellingly moving toward the universal, that has earned, in the relative absence of great German novels, the nineteenth-century *Novelle* the distinction of representing Germany's finest prose contribution to world literature in that epoch.

SYMBOLISM AND THE LINGUISTIC PARADOX

Reflections on Goethe's World View

by

ANDREW O. JASZI

University of California, Berkeley

SYMBOLISM AND THE LINGUISTIC PARADOX

Reflections on Goethe's World View

THOUGH WE OFTEN complain, and rightly so, about the atomization we have suffered intellectually, socially, and morally, it is equally true that contemporary thought, at its most advanced, is striving to replace the concept of entity by that of relationship. The physicist, for example, if he is aware of the theoretical foundations of his science, no longer conceives of nature as being made up of atoms that hang together with each other in time and space, but as a kind of relationship in which there is no room for things that are related. Relationship as being is about to take the place of the notion of being as the being of entities that are related.

It is true, to be sure, that physicists keep "discovering," at an almost alarming rate, ever-new particles that are said to make up the nucleus of the atom, but if they take their own discoveries too literally, they are, I suspect, being fooled by metaphysical presuppositions that are not their own, but those imposed upon man by language in its ordinary uses.

Most languages, including our own, form propositions by connecting a subject with a verb and, by so doing, they impose upon us certain convictions that take hold of our minds with the force of ineradicable or eternal truths. The first of these is that the subject about which we speak, be it a person, a thing, a concept, or anything else, must *be* and be *something* in the widest sense of these words. A tree, for example, about which we say that it grows must be something somehow identifiable as separate from its growth and its other changing attributes. For if that were not the case, if there were no tree, identical with itself, to speak about, how could we speak about it?

If we confront the first linguistic truth, the truth of the subject, namely that being is the being of something, with the second linguistic truth, the truth of the verb, namely that change is the change of something that exists, there arises a problem of immense magnitude. For by demanding that we accept both these truths (being as the identity of something with itself and change as a modification of this same entity) language demands that we do the impossible.

It was this problem of the relationship of permanence and flux, of being and process, which preoccupied Schiller when he introduced the eleventh letter of *Ueber die aesthetische Erziehung des Menschen* as follows:

Wenn die Abstraktion so hoch, als sie immer kann, hinaufsteigt, so gelangt sie zu zwei letzten Begriffen, bei denen sie stillestehen und ihre Grenzen bekennen muss. Sie unterscheidet in dem Menschen etwas, das bleibt, und etwas, das sich unaufhörlich verändert. Das Bleibende nennt sie seine Person, das Wechselnde seinen Zustand.

And a little further below we read:

Etwas muss sich verändern, wenn Veränderung sein soll; dieses Etwas kann also nicht selbst schon Veränderung sein. Indem wir sagen, die Blume blühet und verwelkt, machen wir die Blume zum Bleibenden in dieser Verwandlung und leihen ihr gleichsam eine Person, an der sich jene beiden Zustände offenbaren.

Thus, like so many great thinkers before him, Schiller sought to solve the linguistic paradox by splitting up the subject, the world in which we live, into two halves, an unchanging one and a changeable one, and by asserting that change was merely a modification of the latter, and not of the entire subject. Only the Divinity, in whom *Person* and *Zustand,* substance and attribute, *essentia* and *existentia,* are indivisibly one, and about whom we consequently cannot communicate in the categories of language, is exempt from this division (which I shall call a "horizontal" one). It divides all else, the entire world of language, into two halves, an upper or superior and a lower or inferior one, as it were.

Schiller, to be sure, shared with metaphysical systems akin to his own a tendency to mistake the superior aspect of reality for the extra-linguistic Divinity, *Person* for *das notwendige Wesen* or *das absolute Subjekt*. Nevertheless, this "person" which, like "condition," owed its existence to the attempts of human thought to settle the linguistic dilemma along horizontal lines, is, in truth, not God, but merely one aspect of the total world interpreted by language. I shall, accordingly, also call it the "linguistic absolute" or the "linguistic God."

Schiller's solution of the paradox was unsatisfactory. For however passionately he longed to see change as a true modification of something, as a symbolical revelation of person in condition, person, having been separated from condition in an absolute sense, was hardly able any longer to manifest itself thus. Also, it is true that as long as change is seen, as it was by Schiller, as a change of something, *Zustand,* this changeable attribute of an unchanging essence, must, in accordance with the first linguistic truth, itself turn into something unchangeable the very moment it occcupies the place of the subject in a proposition. If we wanted to account for the change of this new subject, it would also have to be split up into two halves, and so on, endlessly. The relationship between subject and verb, identity and change, the linguistic infinite and the finite is evidently not such that we can comprehend it by postulating that the world is divided up into two halves that have nothing to do with each other. Schiller made a gallant attempt to hold fast to the ancient dream that in the finite process of phenomenal change a spark of the infinite might be revealed. Nevertheless, mankind had to awaken from precisely this dream if there was to be hope for a rational solution of the linguistic dilemma.

Mankind had begun to awaken from this dream long before the days of Schiller. In medieval times nominalism, in long and embittered struggles, gradually won a decisive victory over realism and thus laid the foundation of the world in which, except for a few memorable interludes such as German idealism, all of us have lived until the scientific revolution of recent decades. And since German Idealism is so strangely reminiscent of Medieval Realism in its horizontal division of the world, I hope to be forgiven if, in the present paper, I refer to both Schiller and Goethe as realists rather than idealists and discuss those metaphysical trends that mark the next

step in the solution of the linguistic dilemma under the general head-
ing of nominalism. Nominalism regulates the relationship of permanence and flux not only by eventually abandoning the noumenal
aspect of reality altogether, but also by breaking up the subject of
change, that is the phenomenal world bequeathed to it by realism,
into a countless number of unchanging entities. I shall, for reasons I
cannot discuss here, also refer to nominalism as "vertical" thought.
With its emphasis on particulars and its insistence that the universals
(called ideas in the age of Goethe) far from being the source of these
particulars, are merely concepts abstracted from them, all nominalism, ancient and modern, attempts to solve the linguistic paradox by
teaching us to harden our hearts and minds to what I have referred
to as the second linguistic truth, namely that the verb must imply a
true modification of the subject. Subject and verb, being and process,
will never be able to coexist peacefully unless the truth of the verb
is legislated out of existence altogether. We must not take ourselves
literally when we say of the tree that it grows. What a statement like
this really means, according to the nominalistic view, is that the tree
exists as a countless number of entities which, changeless in their
indestructible self-identity, are merely free to change their *positions*
(but not themselves) in space and, insofar as they are mirrored in
human consciousness, also in time. Clearly, for the nominalist, the
subject of change, the world, must sooner or later decompose into
such changeless entities. For only in this manner can he make sure
that what *is* will never lose its identity and being by having to suffer
a true or symbolical modification.

The nominalist can think of being only in its infinitely fragmented
form as the self-identity and private property of each separate building block of reality. To the realist, on the contrary, the phenomena
do not exist because they are themselves, but they exist and are
themselves inasmuch as they share in what they are not: in the
ultimately one and indivisible idea. With the elimination of the conception of change as true modification, the ultimate entities that
make up reality and in which being now resides share with the
linguistic absolute the attribute of changelessness. But whereas
Schiller's absolute was changeless *outside* of time and space, the

atoms that make up the vertical cosmos, namely the entities that change their positions ceaselessly without undergoing a substantial change themselves, must be said to enjoy a changelessness *in* time and space. And whereas Schiller's absolute was infinite because it was beyond the reach of number, the nominalistic world is infinite because it is composed of an infinite number of finite entities. In a like manner, the realistic conception of totality, predicated on a relatedness of the phenomenal world to its source, has been replaced by a conception of wholeness as a sum-total of parts.

It is the tragedy of Schiller's brand of realism that the forces that constitute language must sooner or later destroy it by demanding, first, an irreversible separation of the phenomenal world from what, within the language of realism, will appear as its existential source (call it God, the absolute, identity, person, idea, spirit, or what have you) and later, in nominalistic metaphysics, by denying the existence of this source altogether. Nominalism, in the last analysis, denies the existence of this source by transposing it (the principle of permanence) into attribute (the principle of flux), sameness into difference, and by indicating how attribute or the phenomenon, now identified with itself, is nevertheless able to change. But even though nominalism represents a necessary development, it is nonetheless true (be it painfully so) that the nominalistic entity, human and physical, owes its existence to an alienation both from the linguistic absolute and from itself, namely from its attributes change and motion. The atom that moves through space in such a manner that its being is not involved in what it does is an image of man who feels dissociated from his own acts. We are, so it seems, no longer contained in what we do because what we do is no longer an expression of what we really are.

That contemporary thought feels more and more inclined to reject this nominalistic atom has already been mentioned and need not concern us further here. We should, however, like to know whether Goethe, whose fundamental concept of polarity brings to mind the particles and antiparticles of our own scientists, credited the symbol with a higher degree of ontological stability than the modern tellers of *Dichtung und Wahrheit,* of *Truth and Fiction,* credit the atom.

Was there according to Goethe such a thing as a symbol? Or, to phrase this a little differently, what sort of thing was the symbol according to Goethe?

II

Whereas the problem facing Schiller was how the infinite which he had separated once and for all from the phenomenal world could be persuaded nevertheless to enter into communion with the finite, it was Goethe's deepest conviction that such a communion existed and that what he had to do first and last of all was to work out the practical details of this relationship. But if we see in symbolism, as Goethe did, a revelation of *Dauer im Wechsel,* of permanence in flux, of *Idee in Erscheinung,* and then stop to ask ourselves whether symbolism is possible within what I have called the world of language, the answer, as the first section of this paper has shown, will have to be an emphatic no. The object about which we speak, the subject of the sentence, owes its very existence to its inability to reveal itself in symbolical process.

The assertion, to be sure, that the subject cannot reveal *itself* in symbolical process misses the point, as far as Goethe is concerned. For in referring to phenomenal change as a symbolical one, Goethe does not have in mind a *self*-revelation of the phenomenon, but rather wishes to indicate that the phenomena, in their ceaseless change, reveal to us a principle of permanence which, at different times and with differing emphasis, he liked to call *Typus, Idee,* or *Gottheit.* Thus, even when he speaks about a particular phenomenon, which he was forced to do by the structure of language and by his passionate love of particulars, he is usually aware that he is not really talking about a phenomenon that changes, but about the phenomenal world of change as the other aspect of permanence. "Es ist alles nur Eins; aber von diesem Einen an sich zu reden, wer vermag es?" (conversation with Riemer, August 2, 1807). Contrary to what seems to make sense, for Goethe, unlike for his friend Schiller, the idea which he called eternal and indivisibly one had an existence only in the countless and ever-changing events that make up the phenomenal world, just as each phenomenon could only be and be so breathtakingly different from all the others because it was one with them in the idea. "Das Höchste ist das Anschauen des Verschiednen als identisch . . ." (MR, No.14).[1] "Die Idee ist ewig und einzig; dass wir auch den Plural brauchen, ist nicht wohlgetan. Alles, was wir gewahr werden und wovon wir reden können, sind nur Manifestationen der Idee . . ." (MR, No. 12).

In spite of all this, it seems to remain true that unless we are willing to accept as religious dogma that identity is capable of revealing itself in change, God or the idea in nature, we will, as already mentioned, have to reject Goethe's symbolical vision. For even if we do not try to distinguish between what can be thought to be true and what can be demonstrated to be actually so, it is evident that in a world where what exists cannot change in a true sense and change cannot be a true modification of what exists, the mere thought of Goethe's symbolism will enter our minds with the same degree of ease as that of a square circle. What then remains for us to do? Not so very much, I am happy to say. For in clearly presenting the problem of the relationship of change and permanence we have already come close to its solution. And we are about to solve it along the same lines as those Goethe followed.

The linguistic conception of being as the identity of something with itself ceases to impress us as an ultimate truth the moment we succeed in tracing it back to its own origins. This we have done when we understand clearly that the subject as something separable from the verb (and the existing entity corresponding to it) as well as the verb as something separable from the subject (change as a change of position in time and space) both came into being, namely into being as self-identity, when the "subject" was denied the possibility of pure change (in the sense of *actus purus*). The word "subject" in this assertion must, of course, appear in quotation marks because there "was" no subject "before it" was denied the possibility of pure change. Nor must we take the word "was" literally because there was no time in which something unchangeable could have changed its positions "before" the act of separation I am alluding to had taken place. And if I say that subject and verb have been separated from

---

[1] Goethe's "Maximen und Reflexionen" are quoted according to Vol. XII of the Hamburg Edition and are referred to by the abbreviation MR and the number of the maxim quoted.

each other by an elimination of pure process, we are again dealing with a statement in quotation marks, because I do not have in mind separation as a kind of division or splitting up of existing entities in time and space, but I mean an eminently creative act to which the notion that there are existing entities owes its origin. "Was in die Erscheinung tritt, muss sich trennen, um nur zu erscheinen."[2] Subject and verb have not been separated from each other, as we must say within the framework of language, but have been separated into existence, namely into that existence, the existence of something that exists, which, if I may say this once again, is the one and only concept of existence in the world of language. The rule of the nominalistic concept of being cannot be contested within language and the phenomenal sphere, for these phenomena would not have been separated into "existence" if we could find among them even a single one that did not exist in the linguistic sense of the word. A creative act of separation, then, lies hidden at the root of the linguistic concept of being as the being of separate things. It is the true being or source of the linguistic concept of being and it is also the source of all those fundamental categories of space and time, part and whole, causality, etc., at which the human mind had to arrive sooner or later if the paradox inherent in the world of being (change as the change of something changeless) was to come closer to its solution.

But the act which separates is also one which unites. For once we understand that the *Doppelingredienzien des Universums* (letter to Knebel, April 8, 1812) which in Schiller's world, for example, are alienated from each other, appear to be separate because they have been separated into being out of a condition when no subject was as yet separable from its verb and which, therefore, we cannot and should not conceptualize, we also know that substance and attribute, "person" and "condition," idea and appearance, are not actually separate from each other, but that, in their separation and because of their separation, they are ultimately and forever one in the creative center and matrix of reality. Because this center *is not* in any linguistic sense, it is the source of all that is.

I am, of course, talking about Goethe's conception of polarity,

---

[2] "Polarität" in Goethes Werke, Sophienausgabe, II. Abt., Vol. XI, p. 166.

which, as he continued ceaselessly to study the relationship of the two aspects of his realistic universe, assumed a more and more central position in his thought. On May 17, 1808, for example, he noted in his diary in markedly Hegelian terms: "Ueber Metamorphose und deren Sinn; Systole und Diastole des Weltgeistes, aus jener geht die Spezifikation hervor, aus dieser das Fortgehn ins Unendliche." "Specification" and "progression to infinity" correspond to "condition" and "person" or phenomenon and idea as Schiller understood these, with the important difference, however, that Goethe is able to see change as a manifestation of permanence and permanence as a manifestation of change (this is what metamorphosis meant to him) because he is able to see both as manifestations of an underlying principle in which they are one. In the letter to Knebel just referred to we read similarly:

Wem es nicht zu Kopfe will, dass Geist und Materie, Seele und Körper. . . . die notwendigen Doppelingredienzien des Universums waren, sind und sein werden, die beide gleiche Rechte für sich fordern und deswegen beide zusammen wohl als Stellvertreter Gottes angesehen werden können— wer zu dieser Vorstellung sich nicht erheben kann, der hätte das Denken längst aufgeben, und auf gemeinen Weltklatsch seine Tage verwenden sollen.

And finally a quotation from Goethe's *Nachlass*:

Der Mathematiker ist angewiesen aufs Quantitative, auf alles, was sich durch Zahl und Mass bestimmen lässt, und also gewissermassen auf das äusserlich erkennbare Universum. Betrachten wir aber dieses, insofern uns Fähigkeit gegeben ist, mit vollem Geiste und aus allen Kräften, so erkennen wir, dass Quantität und *Qualität* [namely: "das Unmessbarste, welches wir Gott nennen"] als die zwei Pole des erscheinenden Daseins gelten müssen . . ." (MR, No. 641)

Statements like the above bring to mind the word "Gott-Natur" that occurs in a famous poem ("Im ernsten Beinhaus war's") Goethe dedicated to the memory of Schiller in 1826:

> Was kann der Mensch im Leben mehr gewinnen,
> Als dass sich Gott-Natur ihm offenbare?
> Wie sie das Feste lässt zu Geist verrinnen,
> Wie sie das Geisterzeugte fest bewahre.

The hyphen between *Gott* and *Natur* connects the two aspects of Goethe's total universe by separating them. It stands as a drastically abbreviated sign for the accumulated wisdom of his life. Within the framework of polarity he was able to account for the nominalistic entities as well as for states of undifferentiated mysticism and could put up with both as manifesting the extremes of contraction and expansion, respectively. But, by and large, we can say that it is the linguistic conception of God whose relationship with the other half of the realistic cosmos the hyphen in *Gott-Natur* regulates. Symbolism, in this sense, meant a revelation of the center of being, of "das Unerforschliche" through the elements of the world as interpreted by the language of realism. "Das ist die wahre Symbolik, wo das Besondere das Allgemeinere repräsentiert, nicht als Traum und Schatten, sondern als lebendig-augenblickliche Offenbarung des Unerforschlichen" (MR, No. 752).

The story of the hyphen between the general and the specific, between idea and appearance, between God and nature, to a large extent is the story of Goethe's symbolical vision and of his life. To do full justice to his conception of symbolism in the late formulations which primarily concern us here, we would have to retell this story in its entirety. Unfortunately, not even a brief summary can be given in the present paper. But in order to understand somewhat better the message of Goethe's symbolism we should remind ourselves, at least in passing, of those days of Goethe's youth, far away now, when idea and appearance which symbolism reunites had not yet been made different and when he experienced the divine oneness of these, and his own with them, as high and glorious adventure; and was nearly destroyed by it. We should remind ourselves of the beautiful passion and pathological literalness with which he demanded and often enough was able to experience a union with the eternal moment. Time and eternity were one, not in the symbolical sense of his old age when the very acceptance of finite time was a guarantee that the moment, instead of disappearing into the dark pit of the past, will in passing, and only in passing, bring a bright message of permanence, but in that primary sense of the oneness of all which will forever fascinate man. And it will forever lead him, unless, like the saint or the mystic, he first divests himself of his finite ego, into death or the lands of magic, as it led Werther and Faust. And we must remind ourselves, most of all, of the first decade in Weimar when Goethe, with unparalleled energy and endurance, labored to free himself of this divine curse and made it possible for us to witness the spectacle of a man being reborn into a world of human dimensions. For it was here in Weimar that the two elements of Goethe's later cosmos, idea and appearance, began their separation into being from the heart of creation and from each other, mysteriously and tenderly, the serene calm of the moon or of the rock and the restlessness of the rushing water or of the human soul still reflecting the light of the holy in taking leave from it. But we should not forget his classical days, either, when the task before him was no longer to be separated and to separate, but to use the discrete elements of his newly discovered reality as beautiful three-dimensional building blocks and yet to build in such a way that each block, in its reassuring separateness from the others, was, nevertheless, a representative of the entire structure. It was primarily in his classical works that the principle of permanence tended to assume markedly linguistic proportions (as *Urpflanze* and *Blatt,* for example) and that Goethe, as a reaction to his early bout with the true infinite, saw in symbolism a question of the relatedness of the two aspects of the human world, without permitting these together to transcend the newly conquered territory. In insisting on these human proportions and in nevertheless experiencing both permanence and flux as something more than language can tolerate, he was drawn into the sphere of the linguistic paradox. He did not know that in attempting to link being and process more intimately than language and even his own classicism permitted him to do, he would eventually have to struggle free from the limitations which both imposed upon him and that a deeper insight into the relatedness of permanence and flux would place him once again so dangerously close to the area of mystery and fascination. Werther's obsession with an infinite from which particulars had not yet been released was, of course, very different from Goethe's late conception of symbolism whose very essence is that it can trace back to the infinite only those particulars which have traveled on the road of differentiation, the road of language, all the way and therefore are able to reveal, in their differentness and because of their differentness, an identity which transcends them. Nevertheless, when Goethe, in his old age, reunited *Idee* and *Erscheinung* with each other in the center, it became evident that it had been the meaning of his life to return to its origins, by leaving them.

III

We are ready now to examine one more of Goethe's statements on symbolism. It is the best known to both friends and students of Goethe:

Die Symbolik verwandelt die Erscheinung in Idee, die Idee in ein Bild, und so, dass die Idee im Bild immer unendlich wirksam und unerreichbar bleibt und, selbst in allen Sprachen ausgesprochen, doch unaussprechlich bliebe. (MR, No. 749)

We note, first of all, that instead of trying to define what a symbol is, Goethe tells us what symbolism does. Symbolism transforms the phenomenon into idea. If we are aware of the distinction which Goethe made between *Idee* and *Begriff*, between idea and concept (the latter is a key word in his definition of allegory), we will understand immediately that all attempts to explain this transformation in nominalistic terms must be futile. A process in which phenomena are compared with each other and eventually subsumed under a common denominator does not represent a progression toward idea but rather toward that dimension of total emptiness and nothingness which we approach as we mount to ever-higher levels of abstraction and which, ultimately, is all that the elements of the vertical world have in common. For once these elements have been produced through an elimination of difference in Goethe's sense (differentiation in its polar relatedness to sameness) and sameness has been transposed into difference as the being of absolutely different entities, we should not be surprised if, by abstracting from all those differences in which being is now located, we arrive at sameness not in the sense of idea but in the sense of nothingness. It is not the function of symbolism but of the entire development of nominalism itself, to lead us to the odd insight that something can, in the end, be defined only as nothing.

But if Goethe's *Verwandlung* cannot be seen as a process of comparison and abstraction, are we to understand that by means of it one half of the universe is simply translated into its other half and is thus free to disappear? We will not make this assumption if we remember that for Goethe a soul without a body was of as little appeal as a body without a soul. And if it is true that nominalism produced a world through a transposition of idea into appearance as the self-identity of the phenomena, it becomes evident that symbolism which, as Goethe's words indicate clearly, is a return to the inscrutable center of being, must reverse this process. Symbolism frees being from its nominalistic isolation and fragmentation. It locates being as idea, the principle of permanence, "above" the sphere of changing phenomena in such a manner that both of them together in their existential separateness represent or symbolize the unutterable. Symbolism thus is a process in which the creation returns to the creator.

"Die Symbolik verwandelt die Erscheinung in Idee, die Idee in ein Bild . . ." The idea which is now being transformed into *Bild* (image), as has just been shown, is not the linguistic absolute, but corresponds to *das Unerforschliche* of the definition quoted earlier. Goethe, of course, knew very well that a world one can talk about, a reality one can comprehend in terms of meaningful signs, comes into being through a separation of *das Unerforschliche* into a principle of permanence and a principle of change, and that, once symbolism has traced these principles to their source, nothing, in the most literal sense, remains to talk about. Where there is nothing identical in either the horizontal or the vertical sense of this world, nor an identity as the other pole of change, language is powerless. This is why we are told "dass die Idee im Bild immer unendlich wirksam und unerreichbar bleibt und, selbst in allen Sprachen ausgesprochen, doch unaussprechlich bliebe." The infinite effectiveness Goethe speaks about is the effectiveness of the symbol as potential creative energy. And because this symbol neither is nor is not in the linguistic sense of being, it is *unerreichbar*: beyond the reach of language.

The preceding paragraph tried to suggest that *Bild*, in its extra-linguistic identity of idea and appearance, might be taken to be the symbol proper. There are two equally valid reasons why it might not. The first one is obvious. We can take Goethe's *Bild* out of the total process of transformation and call it the symbol itself only if we do what, according to Goethe, cannot be done: if we talk about "it." By talking about the "symbol" we convert "it" into something (some thing) that can be talked about. Once we have done this, it is only human to assume that the thing we are talking about must actually exist, not only in our minds, but, say, in a given poem under discussion. Now we are ready to designate the word *Gipfel,* for example, as one of the salient symbols of the poem in which it occurs ("Ein Gleiches") and may wish to add that it forms the nucleus of a whole cluster of related symbols (such as *Wipfeln, Vögelein,* etc.). Having thus made sure that *Gipfeln, Wipfeln,* and *Vögelein* must continue to exist according to the nominalistic conception of being and can no longer take part in the process Goethe called symbolism, we will, perhaps, be assailed by the uneasy feeling that we have done violence to the poem. Somehow, the poem seems so much more "poetic" than the images it utilizes. But we will soon silence our doubts by reminding ourselves that, after all, we are dealing with a poem and that, accordingly, the images under consideration do not simply have to do with ordinary reality (though, in fact, they have to do with "ordinary" reality and nothing else), but, as symbols, designate a reality which is quite special because its elements, like the symbols themselves, function as meaningful signs. Now we will state, in a kind of shorthand, that the word *Gipfeln* stands for (or represents or symbolizes) Goethe's longing for the absolute or Frau von Stein's rather cool attitude toward him, or better yet, because it is the essence of poetry to be ambiguous, that it stands for both at the same time. What we are actually saying is that the sound sequence *Gipfeln* points toward a conception *"Gipfeln"* which, in turn, points toward *Gipfeln* as elements of an imagined sphere of reality which, in turn, point toward abstractions of ever-higher levels and, therefore, ultimately, point toward nothing. Having thus converted symbolism into allegory and having, at the same time, indicated that the poem moves on different levels of meaning and ambiguity, we will conclude that nothingness was the calm for which the heart of the poet longed. This insight, finally, will enable us to classify Goethe as a forerunner of modern nihilism.

If, on the other hand, we listen to Goethe's poem without bias, we will not experience its semantic structure as a sequence of separate concepts in what nominalism considers time, but as change in Goethe's sense, namely as a process of differentiation in which is revealed a principle of permanence, an idea, which we need not conceptualize because it "conceptualizes" itself in the meaningful event of the poem. It does so in the time of the poem which, as a manifestation of permanence in flux, is structured along the same lines as the semantic aspect of the poem. Nor will we accept the vertical interpretation of the poem as a sequence of phonetic units identical with themselves, but recognize it as a true sound change, as an audible process in which a silence makes itself heard which, in its dependence on sound, cannot be explained as an absence of it. By exposing itself to the existential tension between *Idee* and *Erscheinung*, as these terms apply to the semantic, phonetic, and temporal structures, as well as to the tension among all of these, the poem resolves these tensions in the vision of Goethe's *Bild*. If, as interpreters, we insist on raising the question as to what this *Bild* or symbol is (a question predicated on the conviction that the symbol must be something or that such a thing as a symbol must exist) we will, as indicated, reverse the process of symbolization. We will separate idea and appearance from their existential separation (in which alone they can be one in the sense of *Bild*), transpose idea into appearance as the identity of appearance with itself, and, finally, attempting to answer the question how this changeless phenomenon (call it meaning, or sound, or time) can change, we will dismember it again into those parts or existing entities which the poem strives to integrate.

I mentioned a minute ago that there were two reasons why Goethe's *Bild* must not be taken out of the entire process of symbolization and substituted for it. The first of these we already know: that which is itself is not the extralinguistic coincidence of opposites, but their *linguistic* coincidence in the entity or (as I had less reason to stress in the immediately preceding paragraphs) the linguistic absolute of horizontal thought. Goethe's *Bild* is evidently neither the one nor the other. It is neither entity nor is it what Schiller, as we remember, called *Person* or *Idee*. It does, however, in its oneness of *Person* and *Zustand*, of essence and attribute, of inner and outer, seem to correspond precisely to Schiller's *notwendiges Wesen* or, for that matter, to the God of Saint Thomas. To quote Schiller: "In dem absoluten Subjekt allein beharren mit der Persönlichkeit auch alle ihre Bestimmungen, weil sie *aus* der Persönlichkeit fliessen. Alles, *was* die Gottheit ist, ist sie deswegen, *weil* sie ist, sie ist folglich alles auf ewig, weil sie ewig ist" (*Aesthetische Erziehung,* 11th letter). By taking Goethe's *Bild* out of the entire process and by calling it the symbol itself, we either transform the poem into the entities of nominalism or into what seems to be farthest removed from these entities: into God. If we substitute a symbol itself, in this latter sense, for the act of symbolization, we will be led to the inescapable conclusion that the work of art is neither an image, nor a representation, nor even a representative of God, but is, no matter how much this realization may alarm us, God himself.

Goethe would have been dismayed by the claims of what later became known as absolute art that only *Bild* mattered, that only that was worth talking about that could not be talked about, and that only that existed which, according to language, did not exist. He even maintained (much to the annoyance of an aesthetics that drew its principles from absolute art) that the value of a poem lay in whatever was left of it when we transcribed it into prose. By so doing, he did not contradict his assertion that the categories of language do not apply to *Bild,* but merely indicated that, according to him, symbolism is no more identical with its upper roots in an ineffable reality than it is identical with its lower roots in the nominalistic phenomena. Goethe recommended translation as a test, not because he wanted to cut off poetry from Being, but because he wanted to remind us (and also himself) that art (as well as nature) should not try to approach the true infinite except through the mediation of the *Doppelingredienzien des Universums.*

Nevertheless, it would be hard to deny that the destruction of the symbolical universe was, as a potential disaster, already contained in Goethe's own dynamic definition of symbolism. All that future generations had to do was to take Goethe's *Bild* out of the entire act of symbolization and (if they did not convert it into concepts) let it consume all else in its flames. This process had begun already during Goethe's own lifetime (and even before the unknown date of our quotation) when Romanticism lifted the "picture" out of its frame and, proclaiming the oneness of all, strove to abolish all differences and distinctions, all separations and mediations in their "progressive Universalpoesie" (Friedrich Schlegel) and in a universe that kept progressing toward the uniformity of an unstructured mysticism. Later on, it was the Symbolists who took the symbol out of symbolism. They showed a tendency to divide it up into many individual symbols, but nevertheless resisted the temptation of turning it entirely into concepts along nominalistic lines, and were honest enough to admit, in the end, that they did not know themselves what it was they had taken out. Nietzsche took it out and announced that the world was justified only as an aesthetic phenomenon. So did the poets of Neoromanticism. But *Idee* was hardly part of their vision of oneness any longer because most of its substance had in the meantime been used up, as it were, by the members of the opposing camps who had kept busy converting it into the self-identity and being of their atomized world. From a phenomenal sphere which had already been drained of idea, the poets now withheld even linguistic identity. They allowed subject and verb to merge in an effortless and loveless self-transcendence of appearance: a rhythmic and melodic, sweet and melancholy dissolution. Other poets again (as, for example, Rilke in his middle period) confronted the rigid phenomena of nominalism, the isolated *Dinge*, and forced them to surrender their linguistic identity by making them reveal their innermost core in their outermost surface, in a surface, that is, which in its identity of essence and attribute, of inner and outer, of subject and object, was no longer the surface of something that could be named, but the transformation of a thing into the nameless god of pure expression.

It would be easy to show that the aesthetics of Rilke's middle years are fully derivable from Goethe's *Bild*—if this *Bild* is mistaken for the symbol itself, if the symbol itself is mistaken for the work of art, and if the work of art is mistaken for God. In the aesthetics of pure expression we must see the closing scenes of that fascinating interlude which German Idealism began to stage at a time when the world was, otherwise, turning more and more resolutely toward the nominalistic solution of the linguistic paradox. The two aspects of reality which are reunited beyond the grasp of language in the expressive "surface" are the same ones whose relationships remained problematic in Schiller's cosmos, whose unique reconciliation we associate with the name of Goethe, and which, in their unmediated oneness, threatened to take the place of all else already in the days of Romanticism.

Goethe had seen reality as a process whose phases allowed for the production of the nominalistic entities in their seemingly unalterable rigidity as well as for a revelation of the extralinguistic identity of idea and phenomenon which symbolism strives to accomplish. It would have violated one of his deepest intuitions to substitute an entity or a symbol itself for the process in terms of which reality must be understood. Realism, which in its last consequences negates the existing entity in God, and nominalism, which in its last consequences negates God in the existing entity, depend on each other as *Verbinden* and *Trennen,* diastole and systole. This is why symbolism, as Goethe saw it, can reverse the direction of creation only by maintaining it. It is, I think, as true today as it was at the time of Goethe that we, who live in the linguistic paradox, in the tension between the infinite and the finite, can disprove the truth of the subject, finite being, only by affirming it with an ultimate of courage, hope, and love.

TWO MOUNTAIN SCENES IN NOVALIS AND THE QUESTION OF SYMBOLIC STYLE

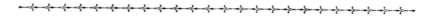

by

J. CHRISTOPHER MIDDLETON

University of London

TWO MOUNTAIN SCENES IN NOVALIS AND THE QUESTION OF SYMBOLIC STYLE

1. . . . Die ganze Gegend ward nun sichtbar, und der Widerschein der Figuren, das Getümmel der Spieße, der Schwerter, der Schilder, und der Helme, die sich nach hier und da erscheinenden Kronen, von allen Seiten neigten, und endlich wie diese verschwanden, und einem schlichten, grünen Kranze Platz machten, um diesen her einen weiten Kreis schlossen: alles dies spiegelte sich in dem starren Meere, das den Berg umgab, auf dem die Stadt lag, und auch der ferne hohe Berggürtel, der sich rund um das Meer herzog, ward bis in die Mitte mit einem milden Abglanz überzogen. Man konnte nichts deutlich unterscheiden; doch hörte man ein wunderliches Getöse herüber, wie aus einer fernen ungeheuren Werkstatt. (Novalis, *Heinrich von Ofterdingen,* c. 1798–1801, Chapter 9)

2. . . . Es kam ihm vor, als ginge er in einem dunkeln Walde allein. Nur selten schimmerte der Tag durch das grüne Netz. Bald kam er vor eine Felsenschlucht, die bergan stieg. Er mußte über bemooste Steine klettern, die ein ehemaliger Strom herunter gerissen hatte. Je höher er kam, desto lichter wurde der Wald. Endlich gelangte er zu einer kleinen Wiese, die am Hange des Berges lag. Hinter der Wiese erhob sich eine hohe Klippe, an deren Fuß er eine Öffnung erblickte, die der Anfang eines in den Felsen gehauenen Ganges zu sein schien. Der Gang führte ihn gemächlich eine Zeitlang eben fort, bis zu einer großen Weitung, aus der ihm schon von fern ein helles Licht entgegen glänzte. Wie er hineintrat, ward er einen mächtigen Strahl gewahr, der wie aus einem Springquell bis an die Decke des Gewölbes stieg, und oben in unzählige Funken zerstäubte, die sich unten in einem großen Becken sammelten; der Strahl glänzte wie entzündetes Gold; nicht das mindeste Geräusch war zu hören, eine heilige Stille umgab das herrliche Schauspiel. Er näherte sich dem Becken, das mit unendlichen Farben wogte und zitterte. . . . Ein unwiderstehliches

Verlangen ergriff ihn sich zu baden, er entkleidete sich und stieg in
das Becken. . . . Die Flut schien eine Auflösung reizender Mädchen,
die an dem Jünglinge sich augenblicklich verkörperten. . . .

(Heinrich falls asleep in his dream and later wakes up) . . . Er fand
sich auf einem weichen Rasen am Rande einer Quelle, die in die Luft
hinausquoll und sich darin zu verzehren schien. Dunkelblaue Felsen
mit bunten Adern erhoben sich in einiger Entfernung; das Tageslicht
das ihn umgab, war heller und milder als das gewöhnliche, der
Himmel war schwarzblau und völlig rein. Was ihn aber mit voller
Macht anzog, war eine hohe lichtblaue Blume, die zunächst an der
Quelle stand, und ihn mit ihren breiten, glänzenden Blättern
berührte. Rund um sie her standen unzählige Blumen von allen
Farben, und der köstlichste Geruch erfüllte die Luft. Er sah nichts
als die blaue Blume, und betrachtete sie lange mit unnennbarer
Zärtlichkeit. Endlich wollte er sich ihr nähern, als sie auf einmal sich
zu bewegen und zu verändern anfing; die Blätter wurden glänzender
und schmiegten sich an den wachsenden Stengel, die Blume neigte
sich nach ihm zu, und die Blütenblätter zeigten einen blauen ausge-
breiteten Kragen, in welchem ein zartes Gesicht schwebte. Sein
süßes Staunen wuchs mit der sonderbaren Verwandlung, als ihn
plötzlich die Stimme seiner Mutter weckte, und er sich in der elter-
lichen Stube fand, die schon die Morgensonne vergoldete. (Novalis,
Heinrich von Ofterdingen, Chapter 1)

I

One of the more notorious German symbolic texts is the "Märchen" narrated by the poet Klingsohr in Novalis' unfinished novel
Heinrich von Ofterdingen (c. 1798–1801). When this "Märchen"
was written profound changes were affecting German ideas about
poetic symbolism. Novalis himself speculated that language could be
made to function as a nonreferential sign-system, like music or mathematics, with the "Märchen" as its principal literary form. He envisaged this "higher language"—*Sprache in zweiter Potenz*—as being
so far removed from ordinary language that it would be autonomous,
an *absolute Kombinatorik*, developed as a poetic corollary to Fichte's
absolutes Denken.[1]

In Klingsohr's "Märchen," the *absolute Kombinatorik* does not

[1] Cf. B. A. Sørensen, *Symbol und Symbolismus in den ästhetischen Theorien*

take effect in the linguistic structure but, if anywhere, in the order of the events narrated. The language is not structurally changed: what it does is to articulate fabulous rather than feasible events, much as Goethe's *Das Märchen* of 1795 had done, though without the ingenuous clairvoyance of actual folk tale. To some minds, the text yields a coherent, if kaleidoscopic, narrative about the coming of a Golden Age. The symbolism pointing this chiliastic way involves some rather arbitrary fusions of stock images and motifs from Greek and Germanic mythology. But it contains also some images which control the play with motifs and make the narrative look at points less like a churning than a patterned confluence of mythic materials. My intention is to trace the lineage of one of these images back into antique roots, indicating what conventions make the image symbolic. I shall then examine the lineage of another aspect of the same image occurring elsewhere in *Heinrich von Ofterdingen*, with a view to making some suggestions about symbolic style in general.

II

The first phase of Klingsohr's "Märchen" opens in a kind of cosmic city which is perched on a mountaintop. Slowly a reddish light, turning to milky blue, begins to flood the city. The streets become visible; throngs of spears, swords, shields, helmets, and crowns appear. Then these make room for a simple green garland, around which they form a circle. All this (I now translate) "was reflected in the frozen sea which surrounded the mountain on which the city lay; and also the distant high range of mountains which encircled the sea was covered to the center with a mild reflected radiance" (*mit einem milden Abglanz*). This paragraph then ends with more description of the city, its sounds, the symmetry of its buildings, the flowers of ice and snow in clay pots by all the windows. I do not know how much significance should be attached to the detail about the events in the city being reflected in the frozen sea. But this detail does intro-

---

des 18. Jahrhunderts und der deutschen Romantik (Copenhagen: Munksgaard, 1963), pp. 201–203. The Novalis *ed. cit.* is Novalis, *Schriften, Erster Band: Das dichterische Werk,* ed. Paul Kluckhohn and Richard Samuel (Stuttgart: W. Kohlhammer Verlag, 1960); extracts to which reference is made are pp. 290–291 and 196–197 respectively.

duce the cosmorama of central mountain, encircling sea, and distant ring of mountains, almost as if it were by afterthought, even with some carelessness in the visual presentation. The cosmorama seems to flash into the paragraph as an incidental detail. Yet it is here that crucial events are to occur; and the cosmorama is ancient. Its original could be the description of Atlantis in Plato's *Timaeus*. But Plato's Atlantis is related in turn to older types of mountain scene. In these older types, too, a structure of concentricity inheres. This appears in the Novalis detail first as the garland with the ring of armory around it, then more significantly in the sea around the central mountain and in the ring of mountains around that sea: like a wheel whose axle is the central mountain on which the city of Arctur stands.

The Novalis detail begins to look like a palimpsest on which recessed versions of a symbolism of the cosmic center can be discerned. Does the Novalis context allow this to be immediately inferred? Yes, but less from the topography given at this point than from a property of the mountain which is soon accented: its being magnetic. We may not find the topography immediately expressive without support from the context because we are dead to its meaningful convention, or because it is an apparently marginal detail. If the second reason is the more obvious one, this could be accounted for by the fact that Novalis was writing before realism entered German fiction and so he could still confidently annex notions and motifs external to a literary work itself without compulsion to establish them concretely in the work: indication was enough, full realization was not necessary. His cosmorama here is not one detail in a symbolism that is contained in its context and analytic in its function, like Kafka's, for instance, in *Das Schloss*, where the topography is not dissimilar, for there, while the Castle hill and the village straggling around it constitute a single labyrinth, the village main street forms at least an indefinitely extended arc, if not a perimeter circling the central enigma of the hilltop castle. Into Novalis' time there had even survived the tendency of later romances to turn symbolic motifs into sketchy stage properties. All the more telling, therefore, is the syntactical arrangement which inserts his mountain cosmorama into full view here: the unemphatic and succinct phrasing suggests at least that here we are not in the presence of mere stage properties.

Now in the *Timaeus*, Atlantis is a mountainous island belonging to Poseidon. Poseidon, for amorous reasons, enclosed the mountain near the central plain with three concentric rings of sea and two concentric rings of land. Later, an acropolis was built on the island, three kinds of stone being used: white, black, and red.[2] The outer wall was coated with brass, the middle one with tin, and the wall of the acropolis itself with orichalcum, "glancing red like fire" (these metallurgic details are varied in Klingsohr's "Märchen"). This city, standing on an oblong plain, was surrounded by an enormous fosse, and, further off, by mountains. Was this plain a high mountain plateau? The text does not say this in so many words; but the other details imply that this was the case. Plato made of this material a political fable; but the material itself comes from oriental sources, in which the same structure of concentricity appears. There are four main sources, from any one of which the material might have come: the Indian holy mountain Meru, and the world-pictures of Sumer, Babylon, and Iran. All these fabulous or near-fabulous cosmic topographies involve mountains. The Iranian one stood immediately behind the view, current in Germanic legend and in medieval Vision literature, that the Terrestrial Paradise, or alternatively a divine city, was on a mountaintop. Possibly Novalis would have known, or at least heard of, certain subsequent modified versions of the antique world-pictures. Their survival into his time was due in part to engravings in alchemy books, like S. Michelspacher's *Cabala, Spiegel der Kunst und Natur: in Alchymia* (Augsburg: 1616), or Libavius' *Alchymia* (1606), or Lambspring's *Ein herrlicher teutscher Traktat vom philosophischen Steine* (1625; Plates 1–3). Novalis is known to have studied such books. It is important that his cosmorama retains the ancient structure of concentricity; this had been lost in most medieval legends, Visions and romances, and it does not (as far as I have been able to find) survive in any alchemical engravings.

The mythic geography of Meru, "central peak of the world, the

---

[2] The color details appear with variants in the original oriental symbolism of Kw'en Lun and Meru, also in Kalmuck folklore of Meru (U. Holmberg, *Finno-Ugrian, Siberian Mythology* [Boston: Marshall Jones Co., 1927], pp. 346–347: see also note 4, below). On Atlantis in the *Timaeus*: J. A. Stewart, *The Myths of Plato* (1904; London: Centaur Press, 1960), pp. 410 ff.

main pin of the universe, the vertical axis,"[3] of which the Chinese had two counterparts, Kw'en Lun and T'ai Chan, is described by Coomaraswamy as follows:[4]

There are seven island continents surrounded by seven seas. Jambu-dwīpa(the world) is the innermost of these; in the centre of this continent rises the golden mountain Meru, rising 84,000 leagues above the earth. Around the foot of Meru are the boundary mountains of the earth, of which Himalaya lies to the south . . . Meru is buttressed by four other mountains, each 10,000 leagues in height . . . On the summit of Meru is the city of Brahma, extending 14,000 leagues, renowned in Heaven . . . About the city of Brahma flows the Ganges, encircling the city; according to one account, the river divides in four, flowing in opposite directions; according to another, Ganges . . . divides into the seven sacred rivers of India.

Of course, folklore all over the world abounds with sacred mountains; J. A. MacCulloch's article "Mountains, Mountain Gods," in *Hastings' Encyclopaedia*, gives ten columns of details. The Siberian versions are related to Meru and follow the same pattern: number and color symbolisms may vary, but it is the same story of a central heavenly mountain, like the more familiar Scandinavian Himinbjorg, sometimes located on the axis of the earth-disc, sometimes actually situated in heaven. One Central Asiatic tale has a rectangular mountain: recalling the oblong plain of Atlantis.[5]

[3] H. Zimmer, *Myths and Symbols in Indian Art and Civilization* (New York: Pantheon Books, 1946), p. 52.

[4] A. K. Coomaraswamy, *Myths of the Hindus and Buddhists* (London: Harrap, 1916), pp. 395–396. On the Central and Southeastern Asiatic elaboration, see U. Holmberg, *Finno-Ugrian, Siberian Mythology,* pp. 346–347: "Round Sumeru there are seven circular golden mountain chains, divided from this and from each other by seven seas. Naturally these seas are also ring-shaped . . . Sumeru itself is shaped like a pyramid slightly broken off at the top . . . The sides of the pyramid facing the different points of the compass glow with different colours. The southern side is blue, the western red, the northern yellow, and the eastern white. These different colours are said to come from the jewel or metal coverings on the different sides . . . These four colours are reflected in the parts of the world facing them, and for this reason the south is called the blue, the west the red, the north the yellow, and the east the white point of the compass." F. D. K. Bosch, (*The Golden Germ* ['s-Gravenhage: Mouton & Co., 1960], pp. 95 ff.) gives further details: Meru as macrocosmic version of the Lotus.

[5] Holmberg, *Mythology,* pp. 341 ff.

The Sumerians, though plainsmen, appear to have actually built their mountain as a sacral center and source of cosmic orientation.[6] In the epic which Kramer calls *Enmerkar and the Lord of Aratta*, come the two lines: "Purify for me Eridu like a mountain, / Cause to appear for me the holy chapel of the Abzu like a cavern."[7] The temple is projected as a symbolic heaven-and-earth mountain, axle of the cosmos; and this mountain plays a rich part in the sacred literature of the Sumerians. The sanctuary, so the same epic tells, was to be built of rocks from mountains; Sir Leonard Woolley's excavations at Ur showed, too, that the weeper-hole drainage system of the structure gave grounds for believing that the temple-as-mountain was covered with earth and planted with trees.[8] The ziggurats at Ur and Nippur were, to this extent, "cosmic mountains," and Eliade writes of them as "symbolic images" of the cosmos: "its seven tiers represented the seven planetary heavens; when he ascended them, the priest was mounting to the summit of the universe."[9]

Mountains, seemingly, were located at the periphery of this other-

---

[6] M. Eliade's *The Sacred and the Profane* (New York: Harper [Torchbooks] 1961) discusses the Sumerian and subsequent sacred mountains in terms of a religious conception of nonhomologous space, which he formulates as follows: "(a) a sacred place constitutes a break in the homogeneity of space; (b) this break is symbolized by an opening by which passage from one cosmic region to another is made possible (from heaven to earth and vice versa; from earth to the underworld); (c) communication with heaven is expressed by one or another of certain images, all of which refer to the *axis mundi*, pillar (cf. the *universalis columna*), ladder (cf. Jacob's ladder), mountain, tree, vine, etc.; (d) around the cosmic axis lies the world (= our world), hence the axis is located "in the middle," at the "navel of the earth"; it is the "Center of the World" (p. 37). Other versions of the axis: Gerizim, Golgotha.

[7] S. N. Kramer, *History Begins at Sumer* (New York: Doubleday [Anchor Books], 1950), p. 23. The Abzu is the "watery abyss," dwelling of Enki, Lord of Wisdom; to him Inanna, queen of heaven, goes to acquire goods for the city of Erech; S. N. Kramer, *Sumerian Mythology* (New York: Harper [Torchbooks], 1961), pp. 64 ff.

[8] Leonard Woolley, *Excavations at Ur* (London: Harper [Torchbooks], 1954) p. 133.

[9] M. Eliade, *Images et Symboles* (Paris: Gallimard, 1952), pp. 53 ff.; also *The Sacred and the Profane*, pp. 40 ff. Dur-an-ki, the name used for the Nippur sanctuary, and others later, means "Link between Heaven and Earth." See also H. Frankfort, *The Birth of Civilization in the Near East* (New York: Doubleday [Anchor Books], n.d.), pp. 56 ff.

wise flat, or even concave, Sumerian earth-disc.[10] When Gilgamesh in the Babylonian epic travels to Dilmun, he has to go through the mountain which bars his way. Then from Dilmun he crosses the waters on his doggéd voyage onward for consultation with Utnapishtim. How much of this topography was explicit in the Sumerian proto-Gilgamesh cannot of course be stated exactly.

The mountain through which Gilgamesh goes in the Akkadian text, according to E. A. Speiser's translation, is a mountain range called Mashu, which means "twins." It is Mashu "which daily keeps watch over sun [rise and sunset] / —whose peaks [reach to] the vault of heaven / [And] whose breasts reach to the nether world below" (Plates 4–5).[11] The Akkadian *Etana* myth testifies that this "range" has its base in certain surrounding waters. Here, when the eagle has carried Etana up into the air, it says: "See, my friend, how the land appears! / Peer at the sea at the sides of E[kur]!" [Ekur in the sense of "world-mountain"]; and Etana replies: "The land has indeed become a hill."[12] Yet the relation between the world-mountain and the Mashu range through which Gilgamesh went remains problematic. This is due in some measure to the complexity of the Sumerian word *Kur*, meaning "mountain." The pictograph represented three mountains. Apart from the normal early tilt, this sign showed no change from the earliest records around 3000 B.C. down to neo-Assyrian around 1000 B.C. But its senses ramified: besides "mountain," *Kur* could also mean "foreign land," "earth," "land," or (like *ki-gal*) "nether-world"; and it also designated the monster Kur, who, like the Babylonian Tiamat, dwelled in the "great below" between the earth's concave crust and the primeval waters under it.[13] "He has gone into Ekur," or "he has gone into the mountain," meant "he is dead"; yet Ekur was also the name of the great ziggurat of Enlil at Nippur.[14] Possibly the iconography on cylinder seals, where the sun

[10] On the disc notion, see Thorkild Jacobsen's contribution, "Mesopotamia," to H. Frankfort (ed.), *Before Philosophy* (Harmondsworth, England: Penguin Books, 1949), p. 186 (published by University of Chicago Press, 1946, under the title *The Intellectual Adventure of Ancient Man*).

[11] J. B. Pritchard (ed.), *Ancient Near Eastern Texts* (Princeton: Princeton University Press, 1955), 2nd ed., p. 88.

[12] *Ibid.*, p. 118.

[13] Kramer, *Sumerian Mythology*, p. 76.

[14] Cf. Pritchard, *Ancient Near Eastern Texts*, p. 436.

god Shamash often appears on one of the twin peaks of Mashu, led to a contraction, in prevailing thought, of the mountain cosmorama into a single two-peaked mountain as an image of how the cosmos was organized around a sacral center.

A reconstruction of the Babylonian world-picture by Meissner clearly establishes its structure of concentricity (Plate 6).[15] Here there is a seven-tiered mountain as central axis; a sea lies between this axis and the surrounding range; and the surrounding range contains the western and eastern twin-peaked "solar gate" mountains used by the Sumerian Shamash. It might look as if Meissner was too systematic; or as if he mistook the notion of a navel-point of creation, exemplified in the ziggurat as symbolic mountain, for a cosmological image in which the earth as such is regarded as a mountain. Yet the latter view does have parallels in Central Asiatic folklore; moreover, it is consistent with several texts. Alfred Jeremias asserted, with an eye on the cylinder seals, that the Babylonian world-mountain was envisaged as being twin-peaked: the two peaks representing the high and the low points reached by sun and moon at the solstices.[16] The identification of solar-gate mountain and central world-mountain is also suggested (though not dated) by a fragment quoted by Kramer (who gives no source): "Mountain of heaven and earth, the place where the sun rose."[17]

[15] B. Meissner, *Babylonien und Assyrien* (Heidelberg: Carl Winter Verlag, 1920), II, Ch. xv, with diagram, p. 109.

[16] A. Jeremias, *Handbuch der orientalischen Geisteskultur* (Berlin-Leipzig: J. C. Hinrich, 1929), 2nd ed., pp. 130 ff. H. Frankfort, *Cylinder Seals: A Documentary Essay on the Art and Religion of the Ancient Near East* (London: 1939), Plate xix (a), described pp. 105ff., also shows the connection. between mountain and fertility. Ea, the water god, is depicted officiating at the liberation of the sun god, Shamash, from a mountain grave. Sargonid seals, ca. 2500 B.C., depict Ishtar at the mountain grave of Tammuz (*ibid.*, pp. 116 ff.). The motif survives into the First Babylonian Dynasty, ca. 2000–1700 B.C. Sacral, cereal, and social levels of the symbol are related by Frankfort in his *The Birth of Civilization* (see note 9), p. 57: "The vivifying rain is also brought from the mountain by the weather god. Thus the mountain is essentially the mysterious sphere of activity of the superhuman powers. The Sumerians created the conditions under which communication with the gods became possible when they erected the artificial mountains for their temples In doing so they also strengthened their political cohesion."

[17] Kramer, *History Begins at Sumer*, p. 88. The parallelism with Parnassus may be no coincidence. Parnassus is not only the Classical Greek earth-navel,

Possibly what we are observing here is the gradual shift from the Babylonian world-picture, with its Sumerian levels still active, toward what was to become the Iranian world-picture. The Iranian world-picture has a definite surrounding range with the center as axis. The surrounding range, Alburj (Arabic $Q\bar{a}f$) includes the highest and holiest mountain range, Haraberezaiti, and the highest peak, Mount Hukairya. The mountain circle is described in several Muslim traditions,[18] and the same idea occurs in the *Hexaemeron* of pseudo-

---

ὀμφαλὸς γῆς, it is also said to be two-peaked (as opposed to "many-peaked," "cloud-capped" Olympus): δικόρυφος, δικόρυμβος, δίλοφος; *bina iuga; Parnassus biceps, bivertex* (Sophocles, *Antigone*, 1126; Euripides, *Phoenissae*, 226 ff.; Horace, *Odes*, II, 1, 39; Ovid, *Metamorphoses*, I, 317). The epithet was adopted by numerous authors of the Renaissance and after, e.g., Spenser, "Virgil's Gnat," St. 3: "mount Parnasse . . . / Doth his broad forehead like two horns divide." Euripides, *Phoenissae*, 270 ff., tells that the supposed two peaks were shared by the brothers Dionysus and Apollo; Nonnos and Lucan repeat this. It is suggested in Pauly-Wissowa, *Real-Encyclopädie der classischen Altertumswissenschaft* (Waldsee-Stuttgart: 1949), XVIII, 4 (article by Johanna Schmidt), that the "shining" of the supposed two peaks, as described in classical authors, might indicate cult worship there—torchlight and sacrificial fires for Apollo and Artemis on one peak, for Dionysus and Semele on the other, unless this attribution was a transference to the mountain itself of the pediment imagery in the Temple of Apollo at Delphi (though Euripides, *Bacchae*, lines 306 ff., says: "you shall see himself [= Dionysus] above the Delphic rocks, crossing the upland between the two peaks"). E. R. Dodds (in his Clarendon edition of the *Bacchae*, 1944, p. 105) subscribes to the view that the two summits were the Phaedriades rocks above Delphi (making Dionysus' hierodrome the Livadi plateau). The question remains: Parnassus has not got two *peaks*, properly speaking. My rash guess is that the conception of a sacred two-peaked mountain could have been transmitted, via Crete, from Syria or elsewhere: Parnassus was said to have two peaks because as a sacred mountain at the navel of the earth it *had* to have two peaks, regardless of actual topography. A Minoan signet ring, ca. 1500 B.C. (*Annual of the British School of Athens*, VII, 29, Fig. 9 [1900–1901]), reproduced and discussed in J. E. Harrison's article "Mountain-Mother," in Hastings, *Encyclopaedia of Religion and Ethics,* shows the Mountain-Mother standing on a single peak, flanked by lions and faced by an ecstatic male worshiper; H. T. Bossert, *The Art of Ancient Crete* (London: A. Zwemmer, 1937), Pl. 503, reproduces a small (13.7 cm) North Syrian ivory relief from Minet el-Beida showing the goddess with corn sheaves in her hands standing on two peaks, between goats.

[18] Discussed in A. J. Wensinck, *The Ideas of the Western Semites concerning the navel of the earth* (Amsterdam: J. Müller, 1916), pp. 5 ff. For Christian ideas about the earth-navel, see C. R. Beazley, *The Dawn of Modern Geography* (Oxford: Oxford University Press, 1897–1906), I, 338 ff.

Epiphanius, with the circle as a barrier protecting earth from the surrounding waters. Here, too, Haraberezaiti or Harati surrounds the earth on east and west (*Bundehesh,* Yasht 19, 1) and also holds in the sea called Vôuru-kasha, which surrounds the earth (*Bundehesh,* Yasht 13). Another mountain, Cekât-dâitik, is also supposed to stand at the earth's center. From this mountain a bridge leads across to heaven (the bridge occurs later in Celtic legend and in medieval Visions).[19] The Iranian cosmorama was a very elaborate one; but it was still anchored in an image of space inherited from Sumer and widely shared among Semitic peoples. Among the latter, too, "sanctuary," "mountain," and "navel" are conceptions which overlap: thus the Samaritan Gerizim, the Iranian Shiz, and the Hebrew Sion.[20] The Iranian cosmorama was also coherent. It became one

[19] F. Spiegel, *Erânische Alterthumskunde* (Leipzig: 1871–1878), I, 191–192. The original of this conception is probably the Sumerian sanctuary Dur-an-ki, Link between Heaven and Earth. Spiegel, *Avesta* (Leipzig: 1852), II, 37–38, n. 4, comments on the etymology of Alburj: "Es ist übrigens merkwürdig, dass vor den Namen Burj das semitische *Ar* . . . Berg, tritt, nicht das érânische *gairi.* Vielleicht ist die Idee von den Semiten aus nach Erân gewandert."

[20] Wensinck, *Ideas of the Western Semites,* pp. 12 ff., also discusses the conjunction of navel, mountain(-top), and sanctuary. The sacred symbolic mountain can be said to "start" at its highest point; here the sanctuary (or Paradise) is located, since at this primal point the cosmogenesis begins. The Samaritans believed that Gerizim was never submerged by the Deluge: "The sanctuary is the type and representation of Cosmos and of Paradise and as such a power diametrically opposed to Chaos; when the Semites maintain that the sanctuary was not reached by the Deluge, this is not only due to the opinion that the sanctuary is the highest place in the world, but also to the conviction that Chaos cannot gain a complete victory over Cosmos; for behind the latter is the creative power of the supreme being" (*ibid.,* pp. 15–16). Cf. George Sandys, reporting on the pyramids in 1615: "The name is derived from a flame of fire, in regard to their shape, broad below, and sharpe above, like a pointed Diamond. By such the ancient did express the originall of things, and that formlesse forme-taking substance. For as a pyramis beginning at a point, and the principall height by little and little dilateth into all parts: so Nature proceeding from one undevideable fountaine (even God the sovereigne Essence) receiveth diversitie of forms; effused into severall kinds and multitudes of figures: uniting all in the supreme head, from whence all excellencies issue" (*A Relation of a Journey Begun An.Dom. 1610* [London: 1615; 4th ed. 1637] p. 127). On the relevant Pythagorean cosmogonic theory, see F. M. Cornford, *Plato and Parmenides* (London: Kegan Paul, 1939), *e.g.* p. 21: "Cosmogony would thus begin with formation of the first solid, probably a pyramid, the fiery seed from which the world is to grow."

source of Western traditions which tell of a mountaintop paradise, or
of a bridge, or again a sea, which has to be crossed before that paradise can be reached (in Latin patristic writings, Paradise often became an island).[21] It is probably from here, and not from Genesis
(which has no explicit mountain site for Eden), that the idea of a
mountaintop paradise was transmitted into Western versions of fabulous topography. Traces of this transmission are found in *The Book
of the Cave of Treasures* (c. A.D. 350?),[22] in the geography of Cos-
mas Indicopleustes, in the encyclopaedic writings of John of Damas-
cus, in numerous iconographic sources (for example, those analyzed
by Ringbom in his book *Paradisus Terrestris,* like the apse mosaic in
S. Giovanni in Laterano; cf. Plate 7),[23] in certain Latin patristic
writings from Bede onward (eighth century); not to mention Dante's
Purgatorio, where the Mountain of Purgatory marks a dense and intricate confluence of oriental, Classical, and Christian motifs (cf.
Plate 8).[24]

[21] Isidore, and the writers who locate Paradise on an island, followed the
Vulgate's *Genesis* translation *ad orientem,* not *a principio,* as location of
Paradise. See C. Stornajolo, *Le Miniature della topografia cristiana di Cosma
Indicopleuste* (Milan: 1908), p. 26. Remoteness rather than altitude was often
a criterion for the Paradise location, once the earlier mountain symbolism had
become obscure, and with the advance of empirical topography. For a useful
synopsis of late Classical and patristic views, see H. R. Patch, *The Other World*
(Cambridge, Massachusetts: Harvard University Press, 1950), chs. 1 and 5.
Isidore himself, in *Etymologiae,* Bk. XIV, Ch. III, describes Paradise as a
locus amoenus, but does not explicitly consign it to a mountaintop. In René
Daumal's marvel story *Mount Analogue* (ca. 1944; pub. 1953; English tr. by
Roger Shattuck [London: Vincent Stuart, Ltd., 1959]), the mountain is itself
an island (like Atlantis in the *Timaeus*). Here there is an ingenious transference of the old solar gate symbolism into a paraphysical frame of reference:
the sun, at the proper moment, penetrates and opens the "shell of curvature"
with which the island-mountain surrounds itself.

[22] *The Book of the Cave of Treasures,* ed. E. A. W. Budge (London: 1927),
this was an early source of the Alexander epic versions of paradise journeys.
See Patch, *The Other World,* "Journeys to Paradise"; also G. Cary, *The
Medieval Alexander* (Cambridge: Cambridge University Press, 1956).

[23] L. Ringbom, *Paradisus Terrestris. Myt, Bild och Verklighet* (Helsinki:
Acta Societatis Scientiarum Fennicae, 1958). Plate 7, from the *Très Riches
Heures du Duc de Berri* (ca. 1410), probably shows a paradise-mountain scene
(not in Ringbom) structurally akin to Iranian versions, though the iconography
is commonly interpreted otherwise.

[24] Patch, *The Other World,* pp. 148 ff.: "By the twelfth century . . . the idea

There was, then, continuity in the transmission of these images, even though the metaphysical sense which they originally symbolized often got lost. Howard Rollin Patch, in his *The Other World*, traces the variety of the grips which the images exerted on men's minds from the third century A.D. on. My sketch suggests a few cardinal details in the remoter background. But does the recurrence of the details in Novalis around 1800 authenticate his "Märchen" scene as one in which a cosmic center is apparent and an active symbol in a poetic narrative? The recurrence itself is a clue, perhaps, to how a poetic imagination works when it is creating symbols, singly or in clusters. (The transmission of symbols, from one conscious recipient to the next, or grafted into a consciousness by some neural accident, is not the question here.) But the recurrence alone is no authentication of the scene as symbolic. I shall come back to this question soon. For the moment I would say merely that an old pattern recurs only if it is born anew and scaled to an original mind's depth of experience; and that such re-creation is here the case. Casual as they seem, the two phrases in Novalis undercut the elaborate intervening advance of geophysical science and evoke in its entirety one of the primal landscapes of the human mind.[25]

III

This evoking was to become a norm of symbolist utterance in poetry after de Nerval and Baudelaire; but during the nineteenth century the subtle aura of association captured by this or that magic phrase became something increasingly less settled within traditional categories of meaning, such as those to which Novalis' mountain cos-

---

of the Earthly Paradise was fairly well established in many respects: it is located in the east, it is cut off from the rest of the world by its high location, or its ocean barrier, or perhaps by a fiery wall, its features are the familiar ones in Genesis described with almost a traditional form and vocabulary" (though, it should be noted, Genesis contains no *explicit* details about a mountain).

[25] M. H. Nicolson, *Mountain Gloom and Mountain Glory* (Ithaca, New York: Cornell University Press, 1959), traces in religious, imaginative, and scientific writings from medieval times to the last quarter of the eighteenth century the gradual move away from mythological attitudes to mountains. She does not mention Blake and Hölderlin, in whom some characteristics of the old attitudes are preserved.

morama was still related. One asks: can narrative fiction effectively confine symbolism to brief deep evocation of this kind? It does not always do so; modern symbolic styles tend rather to sustain or diffuse the moment in which meaning laughs at literal expression. Whole fabrics of symbolism evolve, to carry the complexities of meaning which the modern imagination, at once more realistic and less determinate, rustles from its manifold concrete world. In *Moby Dick,* Ahab nails to the *Pequod*'s mast one of the relatively few coins struck with a mountain scene on its reverse: a doubloon of Ecuador. It is, Ahab says, a "medal of the sun," and it comes "from a country planted in the middle of the world and beneath the great equator."[26] There are three mountains on the coin: Ahab, Starbuck, and Stubb variously apostrophize it, explicating its zodiacal symbolism. And to Stubb, again, it comes to look like the ship's navel—consistent, by coincidence or not, with the old oriental convention in which mountain and navel are both terms for cosmic center. Yet, since the narrative keeps its frontal focus on the ship, its crew and their adventure, the symbolism is braced by solidity of specification in an historical perspective. This is a form of contextual control to which Novalis' symbolic style is both antecedent and in principle opposed. The mountain detail in the "Märchen" is not an isolated one,—a fabric connects that detail and others—but even then, when the hero comes to explore the interior of a mountain in Chapter 1 of *Heinrich von Ofterdingen,* he does this in a dream and in language with a largely lyrical impulse. Here again, whether or not Novalis knew it, myth contaminates the fiction, but in such a way that the symbolism becomes a fiction of feeling, not a cosmological fiction.

In his dream Heinrich lives through an entire tumultuous life and finally comes to a small meadow on a mountain slope to which he has ascended up a dry creek bed. Beyond the meadow is a cliff, and he sees at its foot an opening which looks to him like the start of a pathway hewn into the rock. He walks through, and eventually he reaches a cavern. A great fountain irradiates the cavern with a sort of liquid light. Heinrich strips and bathes in the fountain's basin. The water's touch rouses marvelous images in his mind, and (I now translate)

[26] Herman Melville, *Moby Dick,* World's Classics ed. (Oxford: Oxford University Press, 1920), ch. XCIX, p. 513.

Plate 1: *Multiplication,* from S. Michelspacher, *Cabala, Spiegel der Kunst und Natur: In Alchymia* (1616). British Museum.

Plate 2: *Coniunction,* from S. Michelspacher, *Cabala, Spiegel der Kunst und Natur: In Alchymia* (1616). British Museum.

Plate 3: The "Twelfth Figure," from Lambspring, *Ein herrlicher teutscher Traktat vom philosophischen Steine* (1625). British Museum.

Plate 4: Sargonid seal (c. 2500 B.C.), showing Shamash (sun god) rising from mountain. Frankfort, Plate xix a.

Plate 5: Sargonid seal (c. 2500 B.C.), showing Shamash (sun god) between mountain peaks. Frankfort, Plate xviii a.

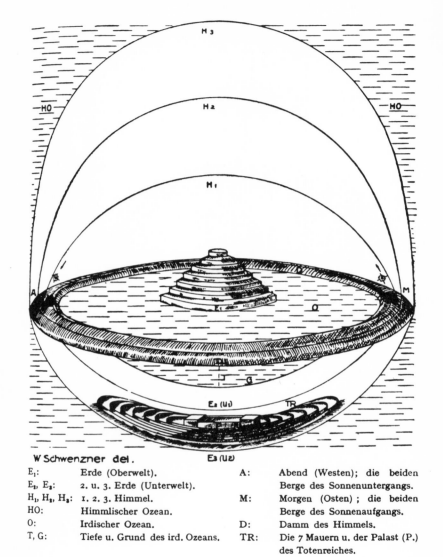

W Schwenzner del.

E_1:	Erde (Oberwelt).	A:	Abend (Westen); die beiden Berge des Sonnenuntergangs.
E_2, E_3:	2. u. 3. Erde (Unterwelt).		
H_1, H_2, H_3:	1. 2. 3. Himmel.	M:	Morgen (Osten); die beiden Berge des Sonnenaufgangs.
HO:	Himmlischer Ozean.		
O:	Irdischer Ozean.	D:	Damm des Himmels.
T, G:	Tiefe u. Grund des ird. Ozeans.	TR:	Die 7 Mauern u. der Palast (P.) des Totenreiches.

Abb. 27. Das babylonische Weltbild (nach einer Skizze von W. Schwenzner).

Plate 6: Babylonian World-Picture, diagram from B. Meissner, *Babylonien und Assyrien,* Bd. 2.

Plate 7: Expulsion from Paradise, from the *Très Riches Heures du Duc de Berri*. Musée Condé, Chantilly.

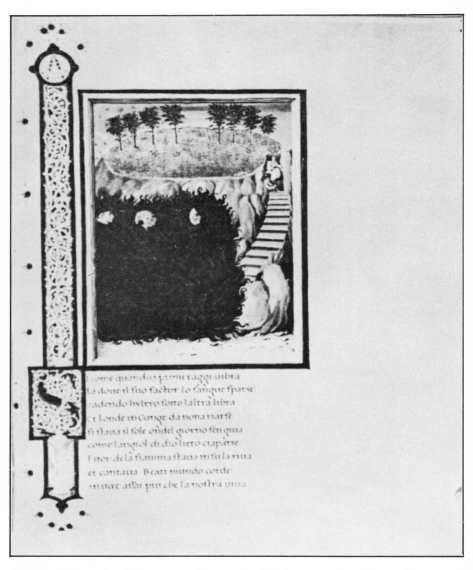

Plate 8: Mountain of Purgatory, illustration (15th century) to Dante, *Purgatorio* xxvii. Vatican.

"every wave snuggled against him like a tender bosom. The water seemed like a solution of charming girls who instantaneously assumed bodily shape against the young man."[27] He falls into a kind of sleep; waking later, he finds himself on soft grass in the open air. Dark-blue rocks with bright-colored veins loom up at some distance; the light is brighter and more mild than usual, the sky dark blue and quite clear. Beside a spring, he sees a light-blue flower with broad shining petals; other flowers of all colors are there, and a delicious fragrance fills the air. Irresistibly drawn to the large blue flower, which moves in response to him, Heinrich sees in its corolla a delicately featured face. At this point he wakes up, roused by his mother.

The dream contains no trace of the uneasiness, oedipal or otherwise, which a Freudian might expect. Its mood is one of marveling delight, of most subtle sensuous enchantment, of passive and unquestioning bliss. The images recall several precedents in medieval Vision literature, where the visionary or dreamer comes to a paradisal place. For instance: the widely known *Vision of Tundale* (middle of the twelfth century), of which Italian, German, Dutch, and English versions exist. Tundale dreams that, after witnessing a mountain purgatory, he comes to a "field of joy and the fountain of life. Here was a door that opened of its own accord, and within was a beautiful meadow filled with flowers and sweet odors, in which was a great multitude of souls."[28] The shared detail is the paradisal field of flowers, which is, of course, a familiar *locus amoenus* detail in Courtly Love literature, and has a rich medieval inconography. In the thirteenth-century *Vision of Thurkel* there are again the purgatory details, followed by details of a great church on the slopes of the Mountain of Joy (=Paradise Mountain), standing in a field which also contains a fountain, over which there grows a tree of great size.[29] The *Vision of Thurkel* also begins in a church, where, from what appears to be a font, a huge flame rises to light the whole edifice. This would parallel the luminary fountain in the cavern in Novalis. Symbolic relations between mountain and temple, and between mountain and

---

[27] Edition cited, p. 127: "Die Flut schien eine Auflösung reizender Mädchen, die an dem Jünglinge sich augenblicklich verkörperten."

[28] Patch, *The Other World*, pp. 112–113.

[29] *Ibid.*, pp. 120–121.

cavern, are normal in the traditional system of correspondences, as Guénon has shown.[30] A medieval instance of this relation is the Minnegrotte in *Tristan.* The Minnegrotte is actually a cavern inside a mountain slope: "gehouwen in den wilden berc."[31] It is possible that Gottfried was alluding here, for all his *ecclesia* allegory, to a Temple of Venus, like the one in the *Epithalamium* of Sidonius, where the temple is on the mountain, though not apparently in it.[32]

For erotic and other antecedents one can go even further back. The Syrian *Book of the Cave of Treasures* (c. A.D. 350), of which the earliest MS is not older than the sixth century, tells how Adam and Eve, when expelled from Paradise, "went down in . . . [hiatus in text] . . . of spirit over the mountains of Paradise and they found a cave in the top of the mountain." Here Adam consecrates the Cave of Treasures, Me'ârath Gazzê, as a house of prayer; but, from what ensues, it would also seem that Eve and he learned copulation there.[33] The Tannhäuser legend, perhaps the best known Venusberg story, with its various folklore versions, is sometimes thought to combine motifs of remote oriental origin.[34] If Andrea di Barberino's story *Guerino detto il Meschino* was indebted to the fourteenth-century Franco-Venetian *Huon d'Auvergne,* this could certainly be argued, since the Turin text of *Huon d'Auvergne* does introduce its mysterious oriental enchantress as dwelling (Cybele-wise) *in* the mountain

[30] R. Guénon, *Symboles fondamentaux de la science sacrée* (Paris: Gallimard, 1962), pp. 218–226 and 261–265 (in the chapters on "Symbolisme de la forme cosmique" and "Symbolisme constructif"). See also Appendix 3 on the Muslim synthesis of mountain and name symbolism, pp. 462–468.

[31] R. Bechstein (ed.), *Tristan* (Leipzig: Bechstein, 1923), 4th ed., XXVII, 16697.

[32] *Sidonius: Poems and Letters, with an English translation,* ed. W. B. Anderson (Loeb Library), I, pp. 201 ff.; Patch, *The Other World,* p. 177.

[33] E. A. W. Budge (ed.), *The Book of the Cave of Treasures,* pp. 68–69.

[34] L. Bechstein's collection of Thuringian legends, *Der Sagenschatz und die Sagenkreise des Thüringerlandes* (Hildburghausen: 1835–1838), contains several tales about people wandering into mountains. Novalis could have known such legends from oral tradition (he was a Thuringian). Bechstein's versions have been styled by the collector, who may himself have been influenced by Novalis. The thirteenth-century Thuringian *Wartburgkrieg* contains a section concerning the cavern of King Arthur; see Simrock (ed.), Pars. 83–84; also F. Mess, *Heinrich von Ofterdingen: Wartburgkrieg und verwandte Dichtungen* (Weimar: H. Böhlau, 1963), pp. 162–163.

—"yn quela montagna."[35] The dark-blue color detail in Novalis has its place in his own color symbolism; but there is a lapis-lazuli mountain in Sumerian sources, for example, the *Song to Martu*.[36] Gilgamesh is evidently the prototype of many subsequent explorers of mountain interiors in Western literature.

Yet there are differences between Heinrich's dream and the older visions and tales of mountains and mountain interiors. Whereas the visions bristle with details of barriers to be surmounted, of ordeals to be suffered, of perilous bridges to be crossed, Heinrich finds what "looks like a path" already hewn into the rock. The earlier part of his dream contained no ordeal of the harsh and spiritual kind which figures in the visions; and the part which concerns us contains no ordeal either. The mountain here is a place not of trial but of etherealization, as indicated by Heinrich's feelings in the fountain. In other details, too, there is a mollifying of tones and contours. The Vision literature tells of violent temperatures, roasting heat and icy cold; but the only time when temperature registers at all in Heinrich's dream is when the light is said to be mild (even that sensation is oblique). And the flower—this is no huge Tree of Life, but an animated plant which responds to the dreamer. In sum: certain points of contact exist between the Novalis dream and the older types; these may be coincidental, as far as one can tell; but when comparison is made one sees that Novalis has none of the dimension of ordeal, anguish, and purgation which the Vision literature, at least, did embody as a dialectical concomitant to the vision of paradise. Without that dimension,

[35] The Berlin text differs: "une dame daleç celle montagne" = beyond this mountain. The "yn" of the Turin text might also mean "on," even though it would have to be "su" to have this sense after about the mid-fourteenth century. The Padua text has "deça de la montagne" = on this side of the mountain (see lines 6672–3 in E. Stengel's text, "Huon d'Auvergnes Keuschheitsprobe," in *Mélanges de philologie romaine et d'histoire littéraire offerts à M. Maurice Wilmotte* [Paris: 1910], pp. 687–713). Other related questions are discussed in W. Pabst, *Venus und die missverstandene Dido* (Hamburg: Kommissionsverlag Cram, De Gruyter & Co., 1955), which names Johannes de Altavilla's eleventh-century Latin poem *Architrenius* as the earliest traceable literary source for the mountaintop dwelling of Venus in post-Classical literature.

[36] A. Falkenstein, *Sumerische Götterlieder* (Heidelberg: C. Winter Verlag, 1959), I.

the dream of paradise is a supreme and radiant fiction of feeling, far from any stereotype, but not consubstantial with the vision.

IV

If this inference is correct, this analysis has shown that fiction-of-feeling symbolism in Novalis ought to be distinguished from the cosmological symbolism which occurred in the mountain cosmorama. Different intensities of imagination have resulted in differing scopes of discourse. Yet such comparisons as these can warp the exegesis and evaluation of texts in which traditional symbols, including radically modified ones, are vehicles of meaning. The worst snags occur when the investigator disregards or misjudges a text's lineage and its internal peculiar intricacies. Myth probers and archetype diviners are known to err quite often because what they find is what they are looking for. My comparisons, which allow for the pervasive tender modulation of Novalis' prose, could indicate that any symbolism which is open-ended and soft-centered can have no more than a sort of detective contact with mythic material, seldom if ever an activating contact, or contact to the core. This might be due to the absence, from such symbolism, of unimpeded give toward objects: it is much more a concentrated vocalization of local feeling. German Romantic symbolism, we know, like much symbolism since, was not structurally suited to functioning as a vehicle of envisioned metaphysical ends— despite its theory. Nonetheless, it has to be realized that Novalis' symbolic style exemplifies that stage in the growth of imaginative genius which Hofmannsthal called pre-existence, occurring in a given man in a definite cultural epoch. He cannot be seriously regarded as an angel marooned on the desert isle of human discourse; but he is also not to be discredited on the grounds that some other style, say Kafka's, authenticates its vision of reality more substantially, or falsifies the stuff of myth correspondingly less.

An historical and comparative investigation of symbolic styles would have little scientific value unless it kept in prospect the discovery of certain laws of symbolic style, even if such laws differed from language to language. Discoveries of that order have I none; but I do have three suspicions: that any symbolic style is unique and inimitable, that the solidity of specification peculiar to the masterly styles is intimately linked with the question of tone, and that poetic symbols are active in a way that others are not, not even the complex traditional symbols in nonimaginative contexts. Tone, as it carries the whole gesture of a style, is at least one factor which makes a style unique, though tone is probably more evasive than factors which are accessible to semantic investigation. Klingsohr begins his "Märchen" in *Heinrich von Ofterdingen* with the words: "Die lange Nacht war eben angegangen;" this "long night" figure is symbolic in context— the narrative proceeds and we find that the night is an aeon of darkness whose end inaugurates a Golden Age: but we know at once that a pretty fanciful story is on the way, and that the fabulous planes of discourse are probably going to evolve independently of any literal planes. The tonal factor is worth emphasizing, because poverty of tone and vaporizing do often consort in writing which, though it may be treating mythic material, treats it usuriously, under the pretext of "shadowing forth" or "expressing" truths called "universal."

But even the tonally controlled presence of universals is not enough to authenticate a symbolic style. Far from it. And the question as to how, by its internality, a poetic symbol differs from any other, is not answered in such technically relevant writings on traditional symbolism as those of Coomaraswamy, Guénon, Eliade, and others. It seems that, because poetic versions of traditional symbols, like the mountain symbol, sometimes resemble traditional symbols outside imaginative literature, their differences often get overlooked. The demarcation lines are hard to draw; a confusion occurs between making meaning and knowing it. It is one of the truisms of the idealist theory of symbolism, where the confusion does arise, that (to quote Philip Sherrard) "the poet, through his use of myth and symbol, seeks to give expression to certain archetypal patterns of experience and to certain universal truths in terms of the particular time and place in which he finds himself."[37] But these stereotype terms, "use of," "give expression to," and "in terms of," show how shakily such argument is yoked to fallacious expression theory. One standard consequence is the view that "poetry . . . is concerned less with the small data of sensory observation or the memory of natural experience, than with the inner

[37] Philip Sherrard, *The Marble Threshing Floor* (London: Vallentine, Mitchell, 1956), p. 242.

nature of life; less with individual vagaries of thought and feeling than with perennial issues."[38] Can this be so? The alternatives are false. For millennia poets have been exploring the symbolizing resources of language not simply for the transmission of meanings ready-made, but for the inaugural making of meaning; and symbolism, in religious as well as poetic language, is a control which makes meaning not via the formula but in a frontal contest with raw existence. Where imagination is at work, making and transmitting are less rigid alternatives than requisite conditions for each other, as *Kubla Khan* shows; but when Sherrard pre-establishes his self-evident universals, he smothers the question of making, and gives a very shallow and schematic picture of the relation between traditional symbols, as registers of the "inner nature of life," and the moment-to-moment life of imagination in the midst of concrete experience.

If we say that literature becomes a form of gnosis only when it is poesis, this does not imply that all poets are incorrigible primitives. All the same, the making of meaning does involve a kind of unknowing (not to be identified with the unconscious). By his intelligence, a poet's unknowing is actually nourished, though, as in Coleridge's case, the system of unknowing can sever its ties with the intelligence it supports. By his unknowing the poet is exposed in the way described by Rilke in his well-known poem, exposed on the "mountains of the heart." It is here that his knowledge can silence the knower who hears the ignorant plant sing. This subtly perceptive and profoundly receptive unknowing could be one source of the internality peculiar to poetic symbols and to poetic versions of traditional symbols: it is certainly a deep motive in the searching discipline of making, as this is undergone by the spirit unappeasable and peregrine. "When great art is spoken of as having universal significance," Philip Wheelwright has said, "we should keep our fingers crossed. What it really tends to have is an eccentric and adventuring *style* of universality."[39]

Philip Wheelwright's own ideas about this eccentric and adventuring style are to some extent corroborated by Wallace Stevens'

[38] *Ibid.*, p. 241.
[39] Philip Wheelwright, *The Burning Fountain* (Bloomington: Indiana University Press, 1954), p. 99.

poem "Credences of Summer." Since this is a theoretical poem about the genesis of active symbols in poetry, we should listen to what it says. All through the poem the phrase "it is" recurs. The phrase has no antecedent subject, and it rapidly comes to sound like a celebration of being, from which soon images emerge defining the complex of perspectives in which imagination and being confront each other. The celebration begins only after obfuscating value-stereotypes like "physical" and "metaphysical" have been purged away with "the hottest fire of sight:"

> Look at it in its essential barrenness
> And say this, this is the center that I seek ...
>
> ... Exile desire
> For what is not. This is the barrenness
> Of the fertile thing that can attain no more ...
>
> It is the natural tower of all the world ...
>
> It is the old man standing on the tower ...

And later:

> It is a mountain half way green and then
> The other immeasurable half, such rock
> As placid air becomes. But it is not
>
> A hermit's truth, nor symbol in hermitage.[40]

In the last sentence, the word "symbol" is pulling negatively against the affirmative recurring "it is." The dialectic of imaginative process involves a nonvital factor which devises verbal make-believe of the kind often associated with symbolism, and a vital factor which creates radical metaphors with ontological status.[41] The poem's seventh section shows how, in this dialectic, distancing and the capture of reality red-handed are interdependent, if successive, moments in a single act of vital imagining. The act moreover culminates not in a statement of the meaning of the object which imagination captures; it culminates in a proclaiming of the "meaning of the cap-

[40] *The Collected Poems of Wallace Stevens* (London: Faber & Faber, 1955), pp. 372–378.
[41] Cf. Wheelwright, *The Burning Fountain,* pp. 93 ff., on "Metaphoric Imagining."

ture"; that is to say, language not merely declaring imagination's arrival at a certain point of orientation in experience, but enacting the whole dynamic of mind which brought it there.

> Far in the woods they sang their unreal songs,
> Secure. It was difficult to sing in face
> Of the object. The singers had to avert themselves
> Or else avert the object. Deep in the woods
> They sang of summer in the common fields.
>
> They sang desiring an object that was near,
> In face of which desire no longer moved,
> Nor made of itself that which it could not find . . .
> Three times the concentered self takes hold, three times
> The thrice concentered self, having possessed
>
> The object, grips it in savage scrutiny,
> Once to make captive, once to subjugate
> Or yield to subjugation, once to proclaim
> The meaning of the capture, this hard prize,
> Fully made, fully apparent, fully found.

The symbol of being as this occurs outside imaginative language communicates itself by other means: it need not be "fully made, fully apparent, fully found." But without this threefold fullness in poetic meaning, the "meaning of the capture" is transmitted only by way of the "symbol in hermitage," the symbol, that is, in retreat from the object and in retreat from being, not dynamic in its condition of exposure to them.

ABSTRACT LYRICS OF EXPRESSIONISM

End or Transformation of the Symbol?

by

RICHARD BRINKMANN

University of Tübingen

ABSTRACT LYRICS OF EXPRESSIONISM

End or Transformation of the Symbol?

I

THE OWL OF MINERVA was not the first to be confused by the question of what "Expressionism" means, nor were the historians of literature the first to become excited about it. The very representatives of that literary era failed to agree on it; some were reluctant to share the same name with others from whom they were separated in certain respects even though they were distinctly united with them in other respects. There are common denominators, both in philosophical outlook and in artistic practice, which for the time being may allow us to use the term "expressionism" as an all-inclusive concept, at the same time as specific and as vague as are other period concepts, such as the baroque and romanticism.[1] One common factor, at least, is the intensity with which all of these people, both in theory and in practice, were concerned with language. Hardly any other period in the history of German literature has wrestled with language with such passion and abandon, not shrinking from distorting and disrupting it in their hectic effort to wrest from language its utmost potentialities, of fully experiencing the bondage and the freedom, the recalcitrance and the pliability, the secrecy and the revelation of which language is capable. Widely different starting positions and purposes lead in the field of language to a fundamentally identical aim: the conversion of that language which everyone uses more or

---

[1] Cf. Curt Hohoff in his Preface to the second volume of the new and revised edition of Soergel's *Dichtung und Dichter der Zeit* (Düsseldorf: August Bagel Verlag, 1963), p. 5.

less thoughtlessly into a language which is no longer the medium of conventional communication and arid concepts, into a language which should become effective through the How rather than the What, and should become expressive through its form as much as through its content. Even where the practical effect on a concrete, social, or political reality is the declared intention, as was the case with the so-called "activist" movement, language, as instrument of programmatic importunity, has a tendency toward the abstract. It exhibits this tendency insofar as it wants to force the public to activate what it proclaims by the very shock of its alienated form and its rhythm rather than by the clear content of its statements. The literature of this period (ca. 1910–1925) seems to lean toward the preponderance of form, toward the abstract, even in cases where it neither wishes to do so, nor declares this as its purpose. Frequently, however, the abstract is the conscious and avowed aim. Again and again the word "abstract" occurs in theoretical reflections on poetry. And those who discuss it or endeavor to realize it in their poems mostly know who their forerunners were. They point to Apollinaire, Mallarmé, Rimbaud, Baudelaire, Edgar Allan Poe, Walt Whitman, and the German Romantics, Novalis in particular as well as Friedrich Schlegel. I do not want to talk about similarities and differences. This would lead us too far away from our subject.[2] In any case, naming these predecessors will give a profile to the German tendency toward the abstract. Problems raised by a poetry leaning toward the abstract are not confined to German literature only, and in German literature not to expressionism only. But within the realm of German Expressionism we find several characteristic, at times extreme, forms and theories which clearly demonstrate these problems.

Nor is the phenomenon of the abstract confined to one single genre of literature. It is to be found in both fiction and drama. Its particular field is lyric poetry, for obvious reasons. I shall limit myself to examples taken from that genre. But I shall not interpret them. That is not relevant to my argument.

[2] Cf. Hugo Friedrich, *Die Struktur der modernen Lyrik,* Rowohlts Deutsche Enzyklopädie, Vol. 25 (Hamburg, 1956).

II

What is the meaning of "abstract?" Everybody knows what this term signifies in formal logic. When we apply it to art, it has a related, though by no means identical, meaning. The poets and theoreticians of expressionism use the word interchangeably with "nonrepresentational." They use these terms in analogy to phenomena of the visual arts, especially painting. However, "abstract" and "nonrepresentational" are not the same, either in poetry or in the visual arts. "Abstract" is the general term, "representational" and "nonrepresentational" are particular terms. "Nonrepresentational" is one possible manifestation of the abstract. What is "abstract" is not necessarily "nonrepresentational," but "nonrepresentational" is always "abstract." I call a work of art "abstract" in which mimesis in the sense of imitation of nature, however wide we may stretch its meaning, no longer remains the prevailing and guiding principle; in which not structure, not the relations and visual integrations of our experience are essentially and fundamentally the organizing factor, but compositional patterns of a unique and artificial kind, not derived from experience. With respect to the nexus of experience and its visual integration, these patterns are devoid of content and for this very reason they are expected to be that much richer in content in the sense of ideas and intuitions. Elements of the nexus of experience, however, may become component parts of these mainly abstract compositional patterns. Paintings of Chagall, for example, one may call abstract: they dissolve the nexus of experience for the sake of an intuitive, intellectual integration, at times dreamlike. However, they are made up not merely of pure forms and colors, but also of patched-up pieces of empirical reality—"vocables of reality" (Broch)—though often changed and transformed. Or: Cubism destroyed the object as "visual unit," or as "optical impression," because it aimed at the *"total* object," projecting "into the picture the spatial and temporal totality of the object." It combines "fragmentary impressions" into a new whole.[3] Also Cubism is not nonrepresentational in

[3] Wilhelm Hausenstein, "Vom Kubismus," *Sturm,* IV (1914), Nr. 170–171, p. 68; quoted from Paul Pörtner, *Zur Begriffsbestimmung der Ismen: Doku-*

the strict sense. Only that work of art is nonrepresentational which is composed of pure forms, not deriving from the total nexus of experience. I repeat: "total nexus of experience," for I do not wish to limit from the start the concept of experience to visual or sensory experience in the customary sense.

Applied to the realm of poetry this means that a work of poetry is abstract when it does not adhere to the generally valid nexus of language, the grammatical and semantic framework of the poet's mother tongue, when it discards its selective system[4] for a new medium of expression. Thus I call a work of poetry abstract when it creates, within the medium of its language, in the manner of its joining and dividing, selection and organization, a new structure of its own. Abstract poetry abandons "linguistic realism," that is to say, it relinquishes that "attitude toward language" which "acquiesces in its actuality as in something given as a matter of course."[5] In other words, abstract poetry aims at statements which, in any manner imaginable, express something different from the conventional system of language and more than it would permit. Poetry wants to escape from its "imprisonment"[6] in language and from the predetermined interpretation of the world imposed by that language. Unencumbered by syntactic and conceptual arrangements of a given language, and in pure forms of expression such as rhythm and sound, poetry wants to express and interpret the world entirely on its own authority. In this attempt poetry remains objective (representational) insofar as it uses as elements of its new compositions disparate "set pieces" drawn from the conventional framework of the mother tongue. "Objective" (representational), in language, means more than "intelligible to the

---

mente, Manifeste, Programme (1961), Vol. II, Literatur-Revolution (Neuwied und Berlin-Spandau: Hermann Luchterhand Verlag, 1910–1925) p. 115.

[4] Cf. Jost Trier, Von den Anfängen bis zum Beginn des 13. Jahrhunderts (1931), Vol. I, of Der deutsche Wortschatz im Sinnbezirk des Verstandes: Die Geschichte eines sprachlichen Feldes (Heidelberg: Carl Winters Universitätsbuchhandlung), pp. 1–26.

[5] Cf. Leo Weisgerber, Die Muttersprache im Aufbau unserer Kultur (Düsseldorf: Pädagogischer Verlag Schwann, 1957[2]), p. 29. The problem of Weisgerber's position will not be discussed here.

[6] Rudolf Blümner, "August Stramm," Sturm, XVI (1925), Nr. 9, pp. 121–126; quoted from Paul Pörtner, Zur Aesthetik und Poetik, Vol. I (1960), op. cit., p. 451.

senses." For that reason, the term should be put in quotation marks. "Objective" can be understood here only in the sense of linguistic realism.

Now, all poetry, whenever it is a work of art, contains a constitutive abstract element. Goethe's poem "Über allen Gipfeln ist Ruh," when read merely as a factual statement, conveys a very simple, if not banal, meaning. Everyone in the street understands it at once, and if he has no sense for artistic values, he won't have any doubts that he could do the same, though perhaps not in verse. What makes this little poem a treasure seems not to be at all rooted in its content, but in something "more," something beyond the margin of what everyone can say. This something "more" is realized only *in* the words and sentences of the factual statement, but it is not identical with them. It is, as we know, the quality we call form or *Gestalt,* including meter, rhythm, sound, image, symbol, and so on. These forms in which everyday speech is more or less conspicuously changed may be called abstract, insofar as they are by themselves not related to any clearly determinable content. But we know that they do have an essential communicative potential resulting from the tension between them and the persistent communicative purpose of each word and sentence of the language *before* they are assigned their function within the poem. We do not wish to consider now this "abstract" element of all poetry. Here the frame of reference of the mother tongue is not abandoned, nor is the way in which the world appears in language given up for a quite different composition of words, but rather both are taken for granted.

III

One should, however, consider forms of transition. Some verses by Brentano, for example, come close to exemplifying the well-known utterance by Novalis: "Poems—simply harmonious, smooth-sounding and full of beautiful words—but without any meaning and correlation whatsoever—only individual stanzas understandable at best —. . . Ultimately true poesy can have allegorical meaning in a universal sense and bring about an indirect effect, like music, etc."[7] A

[7] Novalis, "Enzyklopädie, VI, Poetik" (Fragment 2435), Vol. III, *Werke und Briefe,* ed. Ewald Wasmuth (1943), p. 628.

poem by Clemens Brentano may furnish a suitable illustration:

Einsam will ich untergehn,
Keiner soll mein Leiden wissen!
Wird der Stern, den ich gesehn,
Von dem Himmel mir gerissen,
Will ich einsam untergehn,
Wie ein Pilger in der Wüste!

Einsam will ich untergehn
Wie ein Pilger in der Wüste!
Wenn der Stern, den ich gesehn,
Mich zum letzten Male grüsste,
Will ich einsam untergehn,
Wie ein Bettler auf der Heide!

Einsam will ich untergehn
Wie ein Bettler auf der Heide!
Gibt der Stern, den ich gesehn,
Mir nicht weiter das Geleite,
Will ich einsam untergehn,
Wie der Tag im Abendgrauen!

Einsam will ich untergehn
Wie der Tag im Abendgrauen!
Will der Stern, den ich gesehn,
Nicht mehr auf mich niederschauen,
Will ich einsam untergehn,
Wie ein Sklave an der Kette!

Einsam will ich untergehn
Wie ein Sklave an der Kette!
Scheint der Stern, den ich gesehn,
Nicht mehr auf mein Dornenbette,
Will ich einsam untergehn,
Wie ein Schwanenlied im Tode!

Einsam will ich untergehn
Wie ein Schwanenlied im Tode!
Ist der Stern, den ich gesehn,
Mir nicht mehr ein Friedensbote,
Will ich einsam untergehn,
Wie ein Schiff in wüsten Meeren!

Einsam will ich untergehn
Wie ein Schiff in wüsten Meeren,
Wird der Stern, den ich gesehn,
Jemals weg von mir sich kehren,
Will ich einsam untergehn,
Wie der Trost in stummen Schmerzen!

Einsam will ich untergehn
Wie der Trost in stummen Schmerzen!
Soll den Stern, den ich gesehn,
Jemals meine Schuld verscherzen,
Will ich einsam untergehn,
Wie mein Herz in deinem Herzen!

Here it seems as if the content of the verses hardly matters; as if the manner in which it is presented were even urging us to forget it; as if the poem were almost "without any meaning whatsoever," "simply smooth-sounding and full of beautiful words"; as if the dizzying movement of rotation, an intentional confusion of consciousness, were left, admitting thoughts only in order to dissolve them and to dissolve oneself in deliberate self-annihilation. Yet the medium of musicality which leads us away from the meaning is language, a language which does not overstep the limits of its laws.[8]

A case of transition in a narrower and more delicate sense is the "Phantasus" poem by Arno Holz, who rightly or wrongly is often counted among the protagonists—or is even called *the* protagonist—of German naturalism. When he first formulated his famous art law for which he had searched in analogy to natural science, he meant it to be understood in a dogmatically naturalistic sense: "Art has the tendency of becoming nature again. It will succeed in proportion to the specific conditions of reproduction at its disposal and their implementation."[9] Originally there was little to be misunderstood here,

---

[8] Examples could be multiplied. Principally similar features could be found in the verses "O Stern und Blume, Geist und Kleid,/ Lieb, Leid und Zeit und Ewigkeit," in "Der Spinnerin Lied," in the "Wiegenlied" ("Singet leise, leise, leise . . ."), in the poem "Ach, nimmer will es in dem Herzen schweigen," and in many others.

[9] Arno Holz, "Die Kunst—Ihr Wesen und ihre Gesetze," Vol. V, *Werke,* ed. by Wilhelm Emrich and Anita Holz (Neuwied und Berlin-Spandau: Luchterhand, n.d.) Abt. "Kunsttheoretische Schriften," p. 16.

although nowadays it is fashionable to maintain the contrary. But his concept of nature changed during his arguments with his critics and took on monistic features. Now nature included both the fullness of empirical reality and the artist himself. Yes, nature was both in one. The artist gives shape to the world if he "succeeds in mirroring the reflection which it has cast into [his] 'soul',"[10] as Holz says later. The monumental sequence of poems entitled "Phantasus" on which Holz kept working throughout his life was therefore meant to be as much the "autobiography of a soul" as the biography of nature— both the same. Evolutionary history of nature from its primeval beginnings down to the present of the poet—all its variety was to be rendered in language. Holz strove to accomplish this impossible feat by means of an incredible amount of words, familiar ones, words changed and transformed, and by means of sentences of which some extend across several pages. Here we can disregard the composition as a whole. Only a few lines will serve as example of his manner of presentation.

immer würdesteifer, immer gecker, immer dünkelsteißer, immer
kecker.
immer stolzgeschwollener, immer selbstgequollener, immer
flügelzitteriger, immer federnflitteriger,
immer
gleißglastglitteriger,
immer
schulternschütteriger, immer schwingenrütteriger,
immer
hörnersteilspitziger, immer farbenglutglitziger,
immer halsschilddrolliger, immer nackenkragenkrolliger, immer
kampfpatziger, immer stampfkratziger,
immer brusttiefduckiger, immer bürzelhochzuckiger, immer
schnabelstoßtuckiger,
immer tanztrittknirrender, immer glanzschrittklirrender, immer
schopfkraulkirrender, immer kropfblähgirrender,
immer
schwanzspreitschwirrender,
immer
kehllappenwulstiger, immer stiezsträubschwulstiger,
immer brunstblickzwingender, immer kopfnickschwingender, immer
augenzugeplinktverzückter, immer fittichefauchschleifigverrückter,
immer prachtlustprahlender, immer

[10] *Ibid.*, pp. 87 f.

prunkliststrahlender,
immer flunkernder, immer klunkernder, immer
dahlender,
. . . .
stelzten,
patschelten, hüpften, watschelten, krochen, tatschelten,
nordlandreise—
wanderrastgratschelten,
nordlandreise—zugraststreiften, nordlandreise—
flugrastschweiften,
kreuzquerkrabbelten, querkreuzwabbelten, schnatterrundrannten, flatterrundliefen,
stippsterzsteuerten, schwippschwungstarteten,
glattkleidglitten, pompradschritten,
putzstaat-tappelten, stutzstaat-stappelten, galatracht-tippelten, galapracht-trippelten,
schmuckgefiederprunkten, schmelzgefiederspreizten
und
schaugefiederbrüsteten
sich
Edelreiher, Löffelreiher, Zimmetreiher, Riesenreiher,
Kraniche,
Kampfläufer, Säbelschnäbeler, Strandreiter,
Haubensteißfüße,
Kormorane, Goldrallen, Pelikane,
Sichelenten, Zierenten,
Buntgänse,
Adamantfasane,
Königsfasane, Argusfasane, Silberfasane, Phönixfasane,
Spiegelpfauen,
Perlhühner, Satyrhühner, Hornhühner,
Tschukarhühner
Krontauben, Mennaturteltauben
und
Straußenwachteln!

Here the world of birds is conjured up in words. This is an extremely naturalistic—if you like, impressionistic—maneuver of representation. But—this is the surprising paradox—such a consistent transformation of nature into words, such an overabundance of the concrete, suddenly changes into the abstract. Words and sentences lose their logical and conceptual meaning. They lose their factual, communicative substance. And that which remains is rhythm and sound, accompanied by associations, to which one may or may not succumb. Unnoticeably, statements of fact turn into elements of pure form, which is subjectively determined. Holz thus considered as the core of his poetic principle the relatively appropriate rhythm which shows no regard, and need not show any regard, for preconceived verse patterns or rhyme schemes.[11] Indeed he believed that the structure of his poems and of each individual line was determined by a very strict and exact architectural pattern of numbers. That is to say, by a mathematically abstract scheme of form. Rhythm and mathematical and architectural form are not accidents but fundamental properties of his poetry, and the factual statement which Holz, with phrenetic intensity, seeks to render complete and *fugendicht* (watertight)[12] merely remains a substratum of abstract form. After a hectic fight for recognition, the factual statement surrenders to the abstract, to abstraction, and to the expressive dynamics of abstraction. This can also be stated differently: the abstract form of rhythm, sound, and architectural structure of numbers is the "area of indifference" in which the unity of subject and nature with all their concrete individual phenomena is, or shall be, poetically realized. However, under close examination, the concrete reality of both nature and subject vanishes into something which can no longer be identified; it can be described, but no longer defined. The whole procedure is an enormous linguistic feat, a gesture that can hardly be matched by our empathy, a gesture which, since it aims at expressing everything, conjures up the silence of the abstract. Thus the symbol which, to quote Goethe, is "an image concentrated in the mirror of the mind" because it is "die Sache, ohne die Sache zu sein, und doch die Sache,"[13] appears no longer possible in this kind of "monism."

IV

Arno Holz called his poetry an "art of words" (*Wortkunst*) and he considered the word as an element of rhythmic structure; within an "art of words" the word is the material of a rhythmic and archi-

---

[11] Cf. Wilhelm Emrich, "Arno Holz und die moderne Kunst," in *Protest und Verheissung: Studien zur klassischen und modernen Dichtung* (Frankfurt am Main und Bonn: Athenäum Verlag, 1960), pp. 155–168. The quoted passage is on p. 168. Cf. also Wilhelm Emrich, "Arno Holz—Sein dichterisches Experiment," *Neue deutsche Hefte,* Nr. 94, pp. 43–58.

[12] Wilhelm Emrich, *Protest und Verheissung,* pp. 155–168.

[13] J. W. Goethe, *Philostrats Gemälde, Werke,* Weimarer Ausgabe, I, 49, 1, p. 142.

tectural structure.[14] The term *Wortkunst* was taken up by expressionist theoreticians, especially by the men connected with the significant
periodical *Der Sturm,* founded by Herwarth Walden in 1910. They
did so with all possible consistency. With a certain amount of justifi-
cation they could argue against the protest by Arno Holz that they
wanted something new and something different, indeed the very
opposite of his theory and practice. They were no longer concerned
with nature, neither in a dogmatically empirical nor in a monistic
sense. They were no longer interested in a union of nature and subject, nor in "sensations" which a "sunset" or any other phenomenon
of the material world might "evoke" in the soul of an artist. They
were looking for the spirit, something spiritual, at any rate, for
something which exists only in man, something which constitutes his
nature and his dignity and is supposed to find its "expression" in art.
No doubt, the conception of all this is often quite vague, even em-
barrassingly so, and the "spiritual" element of the expressionists at
times shows quite vitalistic features. Some of them may be called
ecstatic mystics of life. The traces of the nineteenth century have by
no means been completely extinguished. But the fundamental conditions have been changed, essential accents have been shifted.

When Kandinsky, the first painter of nonrepresentational pictures,
in his famous essay on "The Spiritual in Art" (1912), penned the
statement, soon to be quoted frequently, "The word is inner sound,"
he wanted to secede from any kind of naturalistic linguistic usage.
And when Herwarth Walden, in the preface of the catalogue to the
"First German Autumn Salon," an exhibition of modern painting in
1913, proclaimed that "Art is presentation rather than representation" ("Kunst ist Gabe und nicht Wiedergabe"), or when he em-
phasized, in 1917, that "art and factuality are two worlds which have
nothing in common," these statements indicated a new position, at
least for Germany.[15] Even Arno Holz, within limits, could have laid
claim to the first of these statements. It meant, and other expression-

---

[14] Arno Holz, Das Werk, erste Ausgabe (Berlin: Verlag J. H. W. Dietz
Nachfolger, 1925) Vol. X, p. 139.
[15] Pörtner, *op. cit.,* II, 158; Herwarth Walden, *Einblick in die Kunst: Expressionismus, Futurismus, Kubismus* (1917), quoted from Pörtner, *op. cit.,*
Vol. II, 222.

ists have corroborated this, that the logic of art is neither the logic of reason nor that of so-called nature. The artistic mind has immediate insights of its own, its own "revelations," its "inner visions," and for the presentation of these insights it has quite specific media with their specific logic. Already by virtue of its media art is "presentation" rather than "representation." As regards poetry this means that fundamentally it cannot be tied down to grammar or to the syntactic rules of language, nor to its relation system and its semantic framework. In a lecture given in 1917 in the Gallery DADA in Zurich, Hugo Ball said: "The works of modern artists speak in a language known only to them . . . They become creators of new natural phenomena which have no counterparts in the familiar world. They create pictures which are no longer imitations of nature but an augmentation of nature by new, hitherto unknown manifestations and mysteries."[16] This was said in regard to Kandinsky; but Ball, the poet, might in principle have claimed the same for poetry. In an imaginary conversation by Alfred Döblin we read: "I believe that art could dispense even with those subtlest semantic coordinates (that is, the language common to all of us) and, completely unrelated, revel in autarchic neologisms: overcome reality . . . and scorn it."[17] All this does not mean that poetry *must* abandon the rules of grammar. It may use regular sentences and familiar words if they are suited as media for their self-willed statements, or their autonomous compositions, if they "find their confirmation through art."[18] The grammatical relations between words are only "symbols, as it were, scarcely fathomed, of a transcendent logic of language," as another expressionist put it.[19] Thus it may well be that the "images of the art of words are . . . naturalistic, that is, deriving from an optically experienced world," if they are the "expression of an emotion," a "simile . . . for this emotion" and serve the "higher artistic law of formation" (*Gestal-*

---

[16] Hugo Ball, *Die Kunst unserer Tage,* quoted from Pörtner, *op. cit.,* I, 139.

[17] Alfred Döblin, "Gespräch mit Kalypso über die Musik," *Sturm,* I (1910), Nr. 15, p. 119: quoted from Pörtnes, *op. cit.,* I, 171.

[18] Herwarth Walden, "Das Begriffliche in der Dichtung," *Sturm,* IX (1918); quoted from Pörtner, *op. cit.,* I, 410.

[19] Paul Hatvani, "Spracherotik," *Strum,* II (1912), No. 136–137; quoted from Pörtner, *op. cit.,* I, 175.

tung).²⁰ It is rhythm that plays a leading role in this law of form. In it is embodied what may be called *Gefühl* or *Geist*.

The whole of traditional poetry consists, as some maintain, "without exception" of "statements, assertions, and appeals."²¹ Thus it has remained imprisoned in a cage of world interpretation already implicit in language. In opposition to this restriction the expressionists search for a language which once again will fulfill its original task of comprehending—indeed, of constituting—reality, the task of interpreting it anew, establishing a new level in the relationship of man and reality; and this at a time when science and philosophy are relinquishing their traditional conceptions of reality.

V

What is the impact of all this on poetry? I am going to discuss three possibilities which seem typical to me. They must serve for others with which I cannot deal here. I shall also omit Surrealism and DADA.²²

A secret language, by the way, has nothing to do with what I am discussing here.²³ Young Stefan George, for example, constructed such a language for his own use and wrote verses in it:

> ... über die Hügel und Inseln klang:
> Co Besoso pasoje Ptoros
> Co es on hama Pasoje Boan.

This is nothing but the product of translation, expressly conditioned by the relational system of the mother tongue. Its signs have been

---

²⁰ Herwarth Walden, *Einblick in die Kunst,* quoted from Pörtner, *op. cit.,* II, 399.

²¹ Herwarth Walden, "Kritik der vor-expressionistischen Dichtung," *Sturm,* XI–XII (1920); quoted from Pörtner, *op. cit.,* I, 421.

²² Cf. Richard Brinkmann, "Zur Wortkunst des Sturm-Kreises," in *Unterscheidung und Bewahrung: Festschrift für Kunisch* (Berlin: De Gruyter & Co., 1961), pp. 63–78. The present passage is on pp. 76–78.

²³ The following does not deal with the so-called "Nonsense Poetry," whose history and problems were extensively dealt with in a recent analysis: Alfred Liede, *Dichtung als Spiel: Studien zur Unsinnspoesie an den Grenzen der Sprache,* 2 vols. (Berlin: De Gruyter & Co., 1963). There are many common phenomena and problems, not dealt with in the present inquiry.

exchanged for invented signs, that is, in a strictly "pronominal" substitution.[24]

1. The first example is Georg Trakl's "Ruh und Schweigen":

> Hirten begruben die Sonne im kahlen Wald.
> Ein Fischer zog
> In härenem Netz den Mond aus frierendem Weiher.
>
> In blauem Kristall
> Wohnt der bleiche Mensch, die Wang' an seine Sterne gelehnt,
> Oder er neigt das Haupt in purpurnem Schlaf.
>
> Doch immer rührt der schwarze Flug der Vögel
> Den Schauenden, das Heilige blauer Blumen,
> Denkt die nahe Stille Vergessenes, erloschene Engel.
>
> Wieder nachtet die Stirne in mondenem Gestein;
> Ein strahlender Jüngling
> Erscheint die Schwester in Herbst und schwarzer Verwesung.

A poem constructed of metaphors. Metaphors in poetry are certainly nothing unusual. The metaphoric, or figurative, use of language is the most obvious and most fruitful mode of changing and expanding the conception of reality implicit in language without violating or forsaking its universal context. The metaphor can coordinate what in reality is separated. It can reveal or establish connections, analogies, relationships which are not actually recorded in the totality of language. Language permits such coordination, if there exists a common factor uniting, according to its immanent logic, phenomena which are customarily separated, or even contrary or incommensurable, in other words, if there exists a *tertium comparationis*. To speak metaphorically means revealing new relations and units or, to use the idiom of logic, new general terms. This presupposes that the phenomena coordinated in the metaphor are to a certain extent clearly determined in the context of the words and images from which they have been drawn. They have been drawn

---

[24] Cf. Wilbur M. Urban, *Language and Reality: The Philosophy of Language and the Principles of Symbolism* (London: Allen & Unwin, 1951; New York: Macmillan, 1951), p. 407. Cf. also Richard Hönigswald, *Philosophie und Sprache* (Basel, Haus zum Falken Verlag, 1937), passim. The present passage refers to p. 167.

from this context in accordance with general linguistic consciousness and the general knowledge of fields of words and images, on a certain historical level, to be sure, and at times with modification by the distinctness of various groups, for example, social or professional groups.[25] In Trakl's poem there is metaphor of a very arbitrary kind. The metaphoric language of the first stanza may still be understandable from the premises of a general linguistic consciousness. This does not hold, or holds only partially, for the following stanzas. The color metaphors, the *mondene Gestein,* the *Jüngling,* the *Schwester,* the *Herbst,* the *schwarze Verwesung,* for example, can no longer be adequately understood from the immanent world interpretation of language, from its *Seinsbild,*[26] nor from any "familiarity" with "traditional fields of images."[27] I interpret wrongly if I proceed from the context in which the words and conceptions that are joined in the metaphors are familiar to me and everyone else—if I identify them in this manner, reducing them to something known beforehand. Interpreters attempt this wrong path over and over again. The revealing context is supplied here only by the individual poem itself. Certainly, the meaning of *monden,* of *Jüngling* and *Schwester* can be approached a little more closely, if one considers the image fields of all the other poems by Trakl. However, it is only in a very vague and tenuous sense that image fields exist in Trakl's work. Certainly they do not exist as a concrete reality, demonstrable in detail, as in the "tradition of classical lyrical poetry" which "gains enduring insights in the contemplated instant."[28]

Studies of Trakl's manuscripts have shown how the poet, in revising his poems, often changed his images and their metaphoric coordinations, replacing them even by contrary ones. It is obvious that the meaning and the nuances of the entire context with all their associations were changed in this process. Certainly the words and their interconnections can never quite lose the ballast of associations from their fields of language and traditional imagery. Accordingly,

[25] Cf. Harald Weinrich, "Semantik der kühnen Metapher," *Deutsche Vierteljahrsschr. f. Literaturwissenschaft u. Geistesgesch,* 37 (1963), 325–344.

[26] Cf. Jost Trier, *Der deutsche Wortschatz,* Vol. I, pp. 1–26.

[27] Cf. Weinrich, "Semantik der kühnen Metapher," *op. cit.,* pp. 325–344.

[28] Walther Killy, "Gedichte im Gedicht: Beschäftigung mit Trakls Handschriften," *Merkur,* 12 (1958), 1108–1121; the reference is to p. 1110.

the power of imagination and association is a supporting element in the reception of these poems by reader and listener. But the "hermetic" poem of Trakl creates a new nexus which cannot be comprehended under these premises. Everything that is semantically predetermined is but a part, though an effective part, of a composition which, *as such,* constitutes the essential statement of the poem. It is basically abstract in nature. "The music of conceptions transcends meaning," a perceptive interpreter has said. And he rightly quotes the words of Mallarmé that poetry is manifested as "fixation du chant immiscé au langage et lui-même persuasif du sens." It is devoid of all meaning, he continues, which could in any way be grasped conceptually; such poems persuade us of meaning by making room for it. They do not divulge the nature of this meaning. They merely strike chords within us, give directions to our imagination, circling with their images around problems, in particular those problems which are aroused by the consciousness of guilt and transitoriness . . . The configurations are predetermined; the elements of the world cannot be changed. But they may be set in a variety of colors. Ever new constellations are possible; the manifestation of structure justifies each constellation."[29]

In one of his letters Trakl wrote a sentence, frequently quoted: "It is such an unspeakable disaster when one's world breaks to pieces." Against this desperate experience of chaos "the poem is placed, not in order to eliminate the chaos—this is impossible—but to try to tame it," without being able to "posit meaning" through this serious play.[30] This makes sense. But it appears also that poetry of this kind does not admit of symbolical expression. It cannot do so if ever Goethe's statement, quoted earlier, is true that the symbol is identical with the thing symbolized, without being the thing and yet the thing itself, "an image concentrated in the mirror of the mind, and yet identical with the object [behind it]";[31] it cannot do so if it is correct that the symbol possesses a *compelling* double reference to two areas of context;[32] or if it is correct that we may speak of a

[29] *Ibid.,* pp. 1120 ff.
[30] *Ibid.,* pp. 1116 ff.
[31] Goethe, *Philostrats Gemälde, op. cit.,* I, 49, 1, p. 142. Cf. n. 13 above.
[32] Urban, *Language and Reality,* p. 424. Cf. n. 24 above.

symbol (as opposed to metaphor) "when by means of it we embody an ideal content not otherwise expressible."[33] We might be tempted to attribute a symbolic character to the entirety of the composition which carries the statement of the poem. But is not an integral part of the symbol the image, understood as an embodying sign? It is difficult to define Trakl's kind of imagery. One talks about ciphers, but the purpose of encoding which would justify this term in a strict sense is absent. Other proposals are little more exact. I myself do not know an appropriate term for this situation.

2. Let us consider another type of expressionist poetry, August Stramm's poem "Patrouille":

> Die Steine feinden
> Fenster grinst Verrat
> Äste würgen
> Berge Sträucher blättern raschlig
> Gellen
> Tod.

Here there can be no question of metaphors. The poet does not try to escape from the prejudged interpretation of the world in language; rather his endeavor is to force language into immediacy of presentation. Some features in Stramm's poem recall Arno Holz's *Sekundenstil*, his technique of pointillistic juxtaposition. This has been pointed out. But in Stramm there is not the same obsessive will at work which aims at the *Verwortung* of the world, that is, its rendering into language with uncompromising directness. His concern is to give back to the word its *Ur-Bedeutung*, its original, primal meaning, as an early defender of Stramm expressed it.[34] Stramm stubbornly represses any conceptual statement so that he may create with words, on the basis of their rhythmic form, new relations and a new nexus of things. In this process he changes words and grammatical forms. He injects movements, relations, and modalities into language of a kind that a student of linguistic structure would deem infeasible in German. The word shall speak before it is linked in grammatical relations and turned into a vehicle of the world in-

[33] *Ibid.*, p. 470.
[34] Rudolf Blümner, "August Stramm," *op. cit.*, p. 452.

terpretation contained within them. It shall retain the whole wealth
of its potential associations. We shall sense its *inneren Klang* which
grants *Wesensanschauung,* intuition of essence, before it is disturbed
or covered up by the statement system of grammar which, in the end,
all freedom notwithstanding, will receive the word into its predetermined jurisdiction. Thus nouns are turned into verbs, verbs into
nouns, intransitive verbs into transitive ones. With other words the
grammatical specification and function remain altogether unclear,
as is the case, for example, with the word *berge* in our poem.
Whereas in the word *feinden,* for example, we have a condensation
of one or several sentences, we find other poems in which one word
is repeated again and again, appearing in all possible variations and
unfolding itself in the metamorphosis of its grammatical forms. The
poem "Wankelmut" may serve as an example:

> Mein Suchen sucht!
> Viel tausend wandeln Ich!
> Ich taste Ich
> Und fasse Du
> Und halte Dich!
> Versehne Ich!
> Und Du und Du und Du
> Viel tausend Du
> Und immer Du
> Allwege Du
> Wirr
> Wirren
> Wirrer
> Immer wirrer
> Durch
> Die Wirrnis
> Du
> Dich
> Ich!

The theoreticians around Stramm called his procedure of handling
words and statements "concentration" and "decentration." Through
this procedure words and statements were to speak immediately for
themselves without the go-between of conceptually coordinating

sentences. In such a way the subjective conditioning both of *Erlebnis-dichtung*, expressing private experience, and of *Rollendichtung*, representing functions allotted to society, were meant to be overcome. A collection of so-called *Liebesgedichte*, to which also *Wankelmut* belongs, is entitled "Du." An early interpreter of Stramm remarks about it: " 'Du,' this is not Lenore, not Friederike, not Charlotte von Stein, nor Laura at the piano. Nor Daphne, nor Chloe, neither Nymph nor Maenad. Also not pompously Venus Excelsior, Venus Urania, Venus Heroica.—'Du,' this is sex itself, swinging within that curve of deepest knowledge of love which we find again in the Venus of Archipenko. Impulse-rhythms circle and pulsate."[35]

Formulations such as these suggest quite well something of the "vegetative" element in this kind of poetry. The words are supposed to be joined in a rhythm which is formed both by their outward sound and shape and by their *innere Klang*, that is, by the associative denotations which they carry with them from the life of the mother tongue and poetic tradition. Here too the factual is not more than a structural element, notwithstanding all *Verdinglichung*, or transformation into objects, of "psycho-sensory experiences," to quote a recent historian of modern German poetry, who, followed by others, called Stramm's poems "concrete poetry."[36] The same critic also maintains that Stramm's poems are *Verlautung von Gebärden*, transformation of gestures into sounds.[37] Gesture—this seems to me a very fitting expression. However, *Verlautung von Gebärden* can never mean that the experienced gesture was there first and was then transmuted into words. Rather the situation is like this: the gestures find immediate expression in the medium of the word. This reveals a new aspect of the tendency toward immediacy, of which I have spoken. For it seems statements made in such a way do not wish any longer to be comprehensible to themselves, so to speak. They only wish to be performed in a paradox between speech and silence. "Not only the intellect is silenced in these poems," says our critic, "but music

---

[35] Kurt Liebmann, "August Stramm," *Sturm*, XII (1921), Nr. 2: quoted from Pörtner, *op. cit.*, I, 432.

[36] For example, Clemens Heselhaus, *Deutsche Lyrik der Moderne von Nietzsche bis Yvan Goll* (Düsseldorf: August Bagel Verlag, 1961), p. 309.

[37] Heselhaus, *Deutsche Lyrik*, p. 310.

too."[38] This is perfectly correct. With much less reserve than Trakl, whose language still retains the mediator of metaphor, Stramm is bent on the undefined and undefinable limitation of his own "game of language," if I may borrow this expression of Wittgenstein for such a context. Stramm's language performs the act of speaking only in a "pantomimic" manner;[39] but it no longer has a subject that can and will say "This is," "This is this," or "This is so." Stramm has done in poetry what Wittgenstein remarks about the adept in his philosophy (if you allow me once more to tear a formulation from its context): he has "as it were" thrown away the ladder on which he had climbed up, he has "as it were" forgotten the organizing and specifying language in order to use language merely as a gesture; he rejects statements for the mere sake of expression. Where distance is thus blotted out, the "mind" is indeed "silenced."

In such a situation we are led to assume that the realm of mediation in which the symbol and symbolic speech are at home has vanished. To quote Goethe again, where is here "the phenomenon transformed into an idea, the idea into an image, and in such a manner that the idea within the image remain forever infinitely effective and inaccessible?"[40] There seems to be no room left for the paradox of identity and distinction of object and image wherein Goethe sees an essential characteristic of the symbol. "A symbol is always a form of representation, not presentation," an American scholar says, as I believe, very rightly.[41] In Stramm's poetry, however, there is presentation, not representation. Here there exists no double relation to two "contexts of discourse." "Analogical predication," which the same scholar calls "the very essence of the symbolic function,"[42] is no longer a relevant category in this case. Double relation exists in Stramm only insofar as each word is determined by both its position in the language and its traditional image field on the one hand and by the compositional nexus of the individual poem on the other.

---

[38] *Ibid.,* pp. 312 ff.

[39] *Ibid.,* p. 310.

[40] Goethe, *Maximen und Reflexionen,* ed. Max Hecker, Vol. 21 of Schriften der Goethe-Gesellschaft (Weimar: Verlag der Goethe-Gesellschaft, 1907), p. 231.

[41] Urban, *Language and Reality,* p. 469.

[42] *Ibid.,* p. 424.

Here, too, one may use the term "symbolic" only if one is willing to attribute to the composition as a whole a symbolic character. Novalis presumably would have raised no objection against such an attitude. For he stretched the concept of the symbol so far that it may include any variety of form. The discussion of the symbol that has been going on since the Romantic Period has at least revealed the questionability of such generosity.

3. Finally, let us look at a third type. It is obvious also that Stramm's poetry, however greatly it may wish to escape from the convention of language, remains nevertheless tied to certain prejudices as to the conception of reality which are settled in the very structure of the language. This seemed to some of the expressionists as not consistent enough. There were admirers of Stramm, or at least of other poetry of this kind, who were ready to believe that he had led the word back to its *Urbedeutung* and its *Urwert,* its original power and essence, petrified in the course of time.[43] The reality of such power and essence they took for granted, and they also took for granted that there is something like original linguistic sounds, *Urlaute,* as they called them. They became radical and wanted to make poems out of pure sounds, in order to penetrate—and they quoted Rimbaud as authority—"into the innermost alchemy of the word"; in order to break unconditionally the tyranny of a spiritless language.

There are two possibilities. The one is shown in Hugo Ball's poem "Karawane." Again a few lines will serve as example:

> jolifanto bambla o falli bambla
> großiga m'pfa habla horem
> egiga goramen
> higo bloiko russula huju
> hollaka hollala
> anlogo bung
> blago bung blago bung
> bosso fataka
> ü üü ü
> schampa wulla wussa olobo
> hej tatta gorem

---

[43] Blümner, "August Stramm," *op. cit.,* p. 451.

eschige zunbada
wulubu ssubudu uluwu ssubudu
tumba ba-umf
kusa gauma
ba-umf

"Karawane"—the very title indicates that an objective reference is still implied. "I have invented a new kind of verse," Hugo Ball writes, "verses without words or sound poems in which the balance of vowels has been calculated and distributed in accordance with the (expressive) value of the starting line."[44] This then is abstract poetry, and it is not only abstract, but also nonrepresentational. It is poetry moving beyond the ordered world conception of language. But, less complicated and more frank than the poetry of Stramm, it retains a mimetic purpose; it wants to be a faint imitation, a conjuring up into sounds of concretely and sensuously experienced reality. One may imagine, in the sounds of our poem, the dragging step of the elephants, and one has rightly noticed the call of the drover, in *jolifanto* for instance, and other elements of a situation implied in the word *Karawane,* become sensuously expressed.[45] That this is possible within the sphere of the semantically inarticulate is, however, not due to the alleged fact that these sounds and combinations of sounds have the character of *Urlaute,* but it is due to the fact that these sounds in their tonality and their capacity of evoking responses in the recipient subject are predetermined precisely by the part they play in the very structure and context of the language which was to be abandoned. As far as sounds, their pitch and stress, carry any meaning in the poem, or evoke an emotion or an idea, they are able to do so only by virtue of being elements of the articulate language of the poet or, perhaps, as they are rather general, of some other languages. In any case, they remain determined, however vaguely, by the sphere of words and sentences.

This is also true of the other type of pure sound-poetry which has been practiced by expressionists. An example is the so-called "ab-

[44] Hugo Ball, *Die Flucht aus der Zeit* (Luzern: Verlag Josef Stocker, 1946), p. 98.
[45] Heselhaus, *Deutsche Lyrik,* pp. 315 ff.

solute poetry" of "Ango Laina" by Rudolf Blümner. I shall quote only a few lines:

> Oiaí laéla oía ssísialu
> ensúdio trésa súdio mischnumi
> ja lon stuáz
> brorr schjatt
> oiázo tsuígulu
> ua sésa masuó tülü
> ua sésa maschiató toró
> oi séngu gádse ándola
> oi ándo séngu
> séngu ándola
> oi séngu
> gádse
> ina
> leíola
> kbaó
> sagór
> kadó

Here there is no mimetic purpose, no longer any remnants of the factual. So it seems. We have no theme, nor any suggestion as to what kind of feeling is aimed at or into which corner of the soul we are supposed to listen. Nothing is left but a pure composition of sounds. At last we are freed from all reminiscences of the irksome yoke of all-determining language. Not quite, though! Even here the sounds draw to a great extent their capacity of evoking some responses from the life they lead, at least in the language of the listener. Blümner consciously tried to prevent possible associations and reminiscences by choosing sound-combinations which have no counterpart in the given linguistic structures, at least not in German.

It is easy, and a sure way of provoking laughter, to dispose of all this as sheer nonsense, as brain-cracked hocus-pocus. The more so, as there are people who practice sound-poetry for fun. One need only think of Morgenstern and others.[46] If we laugh, we should know

[46] Cf. in this connection Carl Friedrich von Weizsäcker, "Entepente und die abstrakte Kunst" in C. F. von Weizsäcker, *Das Weltbild der Physik*, 10th ed. (Stuttgart: Hirzel, 1963), pp. 246–250. The ambiguity of this species does not

the reasons for it. The fact that Blümner was dead-serious about his poetry is certainly no reason for us to be likewise. However, his experiment is of interest because as a marginal case it clarifies a principle. The abstract, which I said constitutes an element of all poetry, is here not only the dominating but the only vehicle of expression, apart from minute and unwanted remnants of association. The medium is "purified" but the fact has been overlooked that there is no "pure" medium for poetry, that is to say, a medium that is not somehow semantically predetermined. If poetry wants to renounce its linguistic character, it turns into meaningless noise or is transformed into elements of music. What is thus denied to poetry, may be possible in the visual arts, though even there color and form often remain tied to shapes and images of memory, even to their counterparts in language, which cannot be denied its claim to comprehend. Blümner attempts to fuse the expressive potentialities of linguistically articulated sounds, stripped of all semantic ballast, with the expressive potentialities of pure rhythmic structures. One may say that in doing so he has, if not in fact, nevertheless in principle, encroached upon the domain of music, which could do much better what he had hopelessly and desperately attempted to do. However, the equation of his poetry with pure music or irrational song is not quite valid. It is something other than a sort of bizarre score. It is a kind of dreaming in rhythmically arranged sounds. Should Edgar Allan Poe have been right in formulating very broadly, "I would define, in brief, the poetry of words as *The Rhythmical Creation of Beauty*,"[47]

begin just here. In principle it has existed in Germany at least since the time poetry of the type of Trakl's was written. In any case it is still uncertain where the lower boundary against the mere chaotic nonsense should be drawn. One might consider whether the findings of structural linguistics might not lead closer to dependable judgments, that is, whether the absolute boundary might not be found where there are no longer any elements which according to the analyses and definitions of structural linguistics applied to a concrete language can become at least potential elements of a semantic nexus. As is well known, the fundamental linguistic and aesthetic problems, as well as the questions of cognition and knowledge connected with them, have played an important role not alone in modern times, or even since the era of romanticism. This can be amply corroborated elsewhere than in the history of philosophy of language in the narrower sense.

[47] Edgar Allan Poe, "The Poetic Principle," in *The Miscellaneous Essays of*

then such sound-compositions cannot be dismissed offhand from the realm of poetry. Blümner's agglomeration of sounds, as I said, is a dreaming in rhythmically arranged sounds. It is a dreaming before or above all factual and conceptual definition, an expression of undefined spiritual stirrings which it is neither possible nor desirable to define, as is the case with nonrepresentative painting or absolute music. One has therefore compared Blümner's poems with Kandinsky's paintings.

Yet we resist the suggestion of giving ourselves up to a kind of poetry in which all reason is sacrificed to the irrational—an irrational which surpasses all romanticism. We do not believe in such a thing as an original symbolism of sounds. The study of an individual language, and even more so, the comparative study of a number of perhaps very different languages, unmasks as deception the often practiced interpretation of vowels with a view to their allegedly universal emotive values. This deception stems from a rash generalization of certain structural and semantic connections occurring, and perhaps recurring, in individual languages or language groups. Blümner's poetry wishes to hold at bay all prejudices of language, in order to remain wide and open, moving beyond all established interpretations of the world, more universal and more comprehensive than all of them. However, a perceptive critic warned as early as 1919, when he quoted with regard to the expressionistic claim to the absolute: "Qui trop ambrasse mal étreint."[48] The contrary is the result, for the author as well as the recipient of these sound-compositions. They both have no other criteria for any inherent substance apart from the emotional and aesthetic sensation of the moment. For this poetry reposes completely in itself and the individual subject. In comparison with music it also lacks the obligatory objectivity of firm, though variable, structural laws. Only insofar as poetry assimilates at least elements of the mother tongue, does it receive its

---

Edgar Allan Poe, Complete Works, ed. by James A. Harrison (New York: Thomas Y. Crowell, 1902), Vol. 14, p. 275.

[48] Wilhelm Hausenstein, "Was ist Expressionismus?" *Der neue Merkur,* III (1919), Nr. 10/11, pp. 119–125; quoted from Pörtner, *op. cit.,* II, 307. Reprinted in Wilhelm Hausenstein, *Aufsätze und Tagebuchblätter aus fünfzig Johren* (1960).

share in the fullness of reality. Only thus is it able to evoke, even in the most willful interpretation, the whole background of the meaningfully proportioned cosmos, this *Seinsbild,* which language has created and which, in turn, has created language, as our universal possession. And only thus does poetry have its share in the community of human beings and is able to be more than the pastime of the solitary, monadic poet and listener, the poet who even refuses to understand what he is doing. To be aware, how one-sided and conditioned the interpretation of the world inherent in a given language or group of languages is, does not give us the liberty of forsaking the frontiers of this language altogether.

Compared with all other modern poetry in which any morphological and semantic traces of language are still to be found, abstract sound-poetry seems to reveal not only a difference of degree, but of principle. And it appears that poetry cancels itself out, if it wants to skip the fact that its medium is language, and a given language at that, and that its essential and indestructible medium is the image in the broadest sense as likeness and symbol, even if transmuted to obscure metaphor. It is a strange paradox that the most spiritual of the arts, the one that seems most intimately wedded to the logos, remains inseparably tied to the concreteness of the shapes of the human world. Concreteness certainly does not mean only that which is visible and can be touched with our hands. It includes also the realm of feeling and thought, also the realm of dreams and archetypal visions. But it is always, in the broadest sense, something shaped according to the images of our experienced world.[49]

VI

I shall sum up: Abstract poetry arises from a fundamental doubt in reality. One can show how this doubt is connected with social and political facts, and in the field of art and poetry with the consequences of so-called realism. The breaking down of faith in the totality of reality which in the nineteenth century was often artificially sustained and replaced by surrogates, ends the possibility of seeing in nature and the world and its order the image of something

[49] Cf. Richard Brinkmann, in *Unterscheidung und Bewahrung,* pp. 74 ff. "Zum Problem des Sozialen," p. 75.

higher and universal—the manifestation of the idea within the phenomenon—as Goethe, and perhaps some later ones, were able to do. In such a situation language, too, becomes questionable, language which presupposes such faith. In poetry, the breakdown of reality takes place in the breakdown of language. The fragments become building stones of a new reality which the poet has not found in the world, but which he feels driven to create himself. Yet to the degree that the phenomenon, the visible configuration, loses its demonstrative and analogical power, the symbol loses its life, at least the symbol in the sense in which we have been hitherto accustomed to understand it in art and poetry. However, considering the functional concepts of reality in natural science and in other sciences, as well as in large domains of art, I must confess that I would not dare to question that there may well be a new conception of form to which one could not deny the name of symbol, just as little as to those firmly outlined, visible configurations which up to now have claimed it alone.

Modern German lyrics which cannot be understood without the tendencies just sketched, including their most extreme manifestations, appear to be searching again on all fronts for a way back to the image,[50] without being able to restore a totality in which it cannot believe any longer, a totality which, in any case, would look very different from the traditional one. It would be a totality that contained an essential element of the abstract.

In the criticism of expressionistic art mentioned before—it was authored by Wilhelm Hausenstein—we read that "the nonrepresentational element in expressionism has been only relative," that is to say, relative in comparison with naturalism. That element was said to be "full of latent actuality" which just could not be "identified." Modern poetry has not overcome this difficulty of revealing the substance which it represents. Or is it that *we* are failing to recognize it? Writing in 1919, Hausenstein asked: "Who can say today whether an art which at present appears as the hyperbole of a way of painting freed altogether from the gravity of the factual, will not appear some day as the hyperbole of a wholly psychological natural-

---

[50] Cf. the significant subtitle of Heselhaus' book, mentioned in n. 36: *Die Rückkehr zur Bildlichkeit der Sprache* (return to the imagery of language).

ism? Of a naturalism, that is to say, which transfers the object from the dimension of the outer senses into that of intuition? A naturalism which closed the shutters against green and sunlight, only in order to contemplate and portray colors, twisting innards, nerves, and circulation of the blood. Music might become in this process the driving experience, replacing travels, love, or the artist's studio."[51] This was said of painting, but the same question may be asked of abstract poetry. Perhaps the answer rhetorically implicit in the question is false. But it is worthy of consideration, for the interpretation of modern poetry and the significance of the symbol for us will to a large extent depend on this answer.*

[51] Hausenstein, *Der neue Merkur,* III, 310 ff.

* This essay was first delivered as a lecture in December, 1963. In the year 1964 appeared the book by Rudolf Nikolaus Maier, *Paradies der Weltlosigkeit: Untersuchungen zur abstrakten Dichtung seit 1909* (Stuttgart: Klett Verlag). In this book manifold aspects of the phenomenon of abstract poetry are presented, supported by an abundance of quotations and likewise demonstrated in the context of contemporary aesthetics and philosophy. Much of this is correct and useful. However, the fastidious language of the study and its metaphysical profundity scarcely render the fundamental problem any more transparent. The appearance of Maier's study provides no reason to modify any of the above conclusions.

The English version of this article was prepared by Dr. Paul Hoffman, professor of German literature at the University of Wellington, New Zealand.

INDEX

abstract, the: tendency toward, in language of the expressionists, 109–110; as form for literature of 1910–1925, 110; forerunners in use of, in poetry, 110; relation of, to nonrepresentational, 111; meaning of, as applied to art, 111–112, 113; meaning of, as applied to poetry, 112–113. SEE ALSO expressionism; poetry, abstract; poetry, as pure sound

Alchymia: and Novalis, 89

allegory: nature and purpose of, 36–38; relation of, to symbol and metaphor, 37–38; potentiality of, 38–39. SEE ALSO metaphor; *Novelle*; simile; symbol; symbolism

— in *Novellen*: in *The Tempting of Pescara*, 41–48 *passim*; in *Clothing Makes People*, 47, 48; as reinforcement of unity, 48–49; in *Romeo and Juliet in the Village*, 49–50, 51; in *Rider of the White Horse*, 49, 50–51; in *Heretic of Soana*, 58–59; relation of, to symbolism, 61–62. SEE ALSO *Novelle*.

Amsel, Die. SEE *Blackbird*

"Ango Laina": as poetry, 130–134

Apollinaire, Guillaume: as forerunner in abstract poetry, 110

Aristotle: 11

art: abstract form of, 111–112; expressionistic theories of, 119–120; future interpretation of modern expressions of, 135–136

Bahnwärter Thiel. SEE *Railguard Thiel*

Ball, Hugo: on language of modern art, 120; abstract poetry of, 129–130

"Ballad of the Long-legged Bait": 28

"Bateau ivre": 28

Baudelaire, Charles Pierre: as forerunner in abstract poetry, 81; mentioned, 15, 16 n. 11, 97

Baumgarten, Alexander Gottlieb: 14 n. 8

Beardsley, Monroe: 34

Beethoven, van, Ludwig: 14–15

Benn, Gottfried: symbols of, 22; mentioned, 16 n. 11

Bergengruen, Werner: use of symbols by, 49; *Three Falcons* of, as classic *Novelle*, 57–58

Bild (image): relation of symbol to, 77–78; removal of, from process of symbolization, 77–78, 79, 80–81; Goethe's conception of, 78–80; compared to Schiller's *notwendiges Wesen*, 79–80; misinterpretation of, by later generations, 80–81. SEE ALSO Goethe, Johann Wolfgang von; symbol; symbolism

Blackall, Eric: 14 and n. 8

Blackbird (Die Amsel): imagery as "signal" in, 61

Blake, William: 38 n. 14

Blatt: 75

Block, Haskell M.: 61 n. 104

Blümner, Rudolf: poetry of, 130–131

Brentano, Clemens: poetry of, 113–115; mentioned, 57 n. 93

Brinkmann, Richard: on disintegration of language, 5

Broch, Hermann: 111

Browning, Robert: on symbolism, 39, 40

Cabala, Spiegel der Kunst und Natur: in Alchymia: as influence on Novalis, 89

Carlyle, Thomas: 27 n. 18

Cassirer, Ernst: and language, 12 n. 2, 15

Chagall, Marc: paintings of, as abstract, 111

Champigny, Robert: 36 n 9

Chiari, Joseph: 12 n. 2

"Classical Walpurgis Night": 4

Clothing Makes People (Kleider machen Leute): use of allegory in, 47, 48

Coleridge, Samuel Taylor: 33

Coomaraswamy, A. K.: 90 and n. 4

Country Doctor (Ein Landarzt): imagery as "signal" in, 61